Twayne's United States Authors Series

Sylvia E. Bowman, *Editor*

INDIANA UNIVERSITY

John Pendleton Kennedy

JOHN PENDLETON KENNEDY

By J. V. RIDGELY
Columbia University

TUSAS 102

Twayne Publishers, Inc. :: New York

Library of Congress Catalog Card Number: 66-17063

MANUFACTURED IN THE UNITED STATES OF AMERICA BY
UNITED PRINTING SERVICES, INC.
NEW HAVEN, CONN.

To Eelje

Preface

THE SEVENTY-FIVE YEARS through which John Pendleton Kennedy lived—1795 to 1870—were span enough to witness the growth of a stripling agrarian nation into a great industrial power and see America's writers develop from feeble imitation to strong individual creativity. As businessman, politician, and author, Kennedy contributed creditably both to the chronicle of material progress and the literary record. His efforts were widely recognized in his own day, and the deserved memorial marker was raised to his career in 1871 when Henry T. Tuckerman, his friend and executor, published an "official" biography and edited the only collected set of his writings. Since that date, however, attention to Kennedy has been only sporadic. It is true that his three principal works of fiction—*Swallow Barn, Horse-Shoe Robinson,* and *Rob of the Bowl*—have occasionally been reprinted, and segments of the first or second book are sometimes included in the more comprehensive anthologies of American writing. But until comparatively recently his creative work has not been re-examined with much insight into its peculiar merits.

Modern revaluation of Kennedy began in 1927 when Vernon L. Parrington published a trenchant analysis in the second volume of his *Main Currents in American Thought.* Parrington rediscovered cultural values in Kennedy's fiction, praised his *Quodlibet* as one of the best of American political satires, and expressed surprise that he had been so long neglected by our literary historians. A few years later, in 1931, Edward M. Gwathmey offered a brief biographical and critical study which, unfortunately, was flawed by factual inaccuracies. Kennedy's two most popular books were also resurrected during this period: *Swallow Barn* in 1929, with an introduction by Jay B. Hubbell; and *Horse-Shoe Robinson* in 1937, with a scholarly apparatus supplied by Ernest E. Leisy. Both works were now often included on the reading lists of courses surveying the development of American fiction.

Van Wyck Brooks devoted a few graceful sentences to Kennedy in his *The World of Washington Irving* (1944), but it was Alexander Cowie's *The Rise of the American Novel* (1948) which furnished the first useful critical summation since Parrington's. In 1954 Professor Hubbell brought his unmatched understanding of the ante-bellum Southern scene to bear on Kennedy in a section of his massive study, *The South in American Literature, 1607-1900.* Yet it was not until 1961, when Charles H. Bohner published his *John Pendleton Kennedy: Gentleman from Baltimore*, that readers and students were finally supplied with an adequate biography. Bohner made full use of the invaluable collection of manuscripts and other documents which Kennedy had left to the Peabody Institute Library, in Baltimore, Maryland; Bohner's book, nevertheless, is concerned much more with Kennedy the politician and the business figure than it is with Kennedy the litterateur. The facts of Kennedy's active public life justified such an emphasis on Bohner's part, but literary critics still acknowledged the need for a fuller discussion of the creative writer.

Recently two unpublished doctoral dissertations have attempted to redress the balance. William S. Osborne's *John Pendleton Kennedy: A Study of his Literary Career* (Columbia University, 1960) covers much the same ground as Bohner's book; however, it includes long commentaries on the works of fiction and other writings. Wallace Leonard Pretzer made a study of sources his special field of inquiry in his *Eighteenth-Century Literary Conventions in the Fictional Style of John Pendleton Kennedy* (University of Michigan, 1963). And mention should be made here, too, of the provocative discussion of Kennedy's contributions to national legend in William R. Taylor's *Cavalier and Yankee* (1961)—perhaps the most fruitful approach yet suggested.

However, in spite of the value of these newer studies in bringing Kennedy's books once more to notice, none has dealt rigorously enough with some of the most revealing questions which can be asked about Kennedy the author. What was his concept of the function of fiction? What impelled him to set each of his stories in a different locale and at a different period of American history? How did these books view the development of our democratic society? How may they be most usefully assessed for the present-day reader? In the study which follows I have tried to explore these and other basic problems. I have mentioned Kennedy's writings which appear to me to be essential to an evaluation of his craft. But, because I believe that his reputation must rest principally on his three long works of fiction, I have devoted the greater part of my book to analytical chapters on *Swallow Barn, Horse-Shoe Robinson,* and *Rob of the Bowl.*

I wish to emphasize that I am concerned in this book only with Kennedy as a literary figure. I have not tried to write a biography, a history of his times, or a fully documented record of his relationships with other authors of the day. I have attempted, however, to provide enough biographical and historical information to elucidate the circumstances of the composition of each of his books. For this background I have drawn as often as possible directly on the mass of documents preserved among the Kennedy Papers. Some of the materials which I have used have been published in whole or in part by Tuckerman and/or Bohner or incorporated in the unpublished studies; other quoted material is here printed for the first time. Since I have found that published versions do not always agree with my readings of the manuscripts, I have made my own transcriptions; and I have confined my editing to the minimum required for comprehensibility. I have reproduced Kennedy's own spelling and punctuation and have supplied only the matter enclosed in brackets.

I have concluded that Kennedy as an author is to be remembered primarily for his contributions as a maker of national legend and for his presentation of the baffling social and cultural problems which the American experiment had created by the decade of the 1830's. Not entirely unexpectedly, I have found that the often expressed views about his "realism" and his "historical accuracy" are largely irrelevant to the proper comprehension of his books—books that are far more often, I believe, free fantasy and unconscious personal revelation than sober documentation of the past. I hope only that my approach may offer some new ideas as to what Kennedy's tales are "really about."

I would like to express my gratitude to Mr. Frank N. Jones, director of the Peabody Institute Library, for granting me permission to quote from the Kennedy Papers; and to Mr. P. W. Filby, assistant director, for aiding me in my study of them. They and their staff have admirably kept alive the spirit of generosity and helpfulness to other authors which characterized John Pendleton Kennedy himself.

J. V. RIDGELY

Columbia University

Contents

Chronology

1795 John Pendleton Kennedy born October 25 in Baltimore, Maryland, eldest son of John Kennedy, an immigrant from Ireland; and Nancy Pendleton Kennedy, member of an old Virginia family.

1800-1809 Attended private schools in Baltimore.

1809-1812 Attended Baltimore College; began writing essays and other creative work.

1813-1814 Served with the United Volunteers of the Fifth Regiment of Maryland Militia during War of 1812; studied law when off duty.

1816 Admitted to the bar; published the "Swiss Traveller" sketches in the *Portico,* a Baltimore periodical.

1819 Visited South Carolina, where he met the prototype of the fictional Horse Shoe Robinson.

1819-1821 Contributed to the *Red Book,* satirical periodical published in Baltimore.

1820-1823 Served in Maryland House of Delegates, identifying himself with Baltimore commercial interests.

1823 Appointed Secretary of American Legation to Chile, but resigned post before the mission left.

1824 Married Mary Tenant, daughter of a wealthy Baltimore merchant; she died in childbirth in same year.

1826 Defeated in race for United States House of Representatives; returned to practice of law.

1829 Married Elizabeth Gray, daughter of a local well-to-do textile manufacturer; began to write *Swallow Barn.*

1832 Published *Swallow Barn;* met Washington Irving.

1833 Served as a judge in Baltimore literary contest in which Edgar Allan Poe was awarded first prize.

1835 Admitted to practice before United States Supreme Court; published *Horse-Shoe Robinson.*

1838 Elected to United States House of Representatives, after losing in previous year; published *Rob of the Bowl.*

1839 Defeated in race to keep House seat.

1840 Published *Quodlibet;* met William Gilmore Simms.

1841-1845 Again served as staunch Whig in House of Representatives; was defeated at end of two terms.

1844 Published *Defense of the Whigs.*

1846 Elected to Maryland House of Delegates and named Speaker.

1847 Defeated in attempt to regain seat in United States House.

1849 Published the *Life of William Wirt.*

1850 Elected Provost of University of Maryland and given degree of Doctor of Laws; made brief Western tour.

1851-1854 Published revised editions of *Swallow Barn, Horse-Shoe Robinson,* and *Rob of the Bowl.*

1852 Renewed friendship with Irving; appointed Secretary of the Navy by President Fillmore (during his eight-month tenure, Kennedy was associated with Perry's voyage to Japan and the search for the explorer Sir John Franklin).

1853 Met Thackeray during the English author's American lecture tour; traveled with Irving in Virginia.

1854 Helped to organize the Peabody Institute in Baltimore; accepted presidency of Northern Central Railroad Company; toured South with former President Fillmore.

1856-1858 Made two tours of Europe.

1860 Published *The Border States.*

1860-1870 Served as second president of Peabody Institute.

1861-1865 Remained loyal to Union during Civil War, an act which cost him friendships in Baltimore.

1863 Given Doctor of Laws degree by Harvard College.

1864 Took first communion in Episcopal Church, to which his wife belonged.

1865 Published *Mr. Ambrose's Letters on the Rebellion.*

1866-1868 Visited Cuba for health in 1866; then toured Europe again.

1870 Died August 18 in Newport, Rhode Island; buried in Greenmount Cemetery, Baltimore.

John Pendleton Kennedy

CHAPTER *1*

A Choice of Life

IN THE PREAMBLE to a last will and testament dated October 25, 1845, John Pendleton Kennedy cast a complacent glance back over the first half-century of a busy life. "I have reason," he wrote,

> to thank God for many blessings: for kind friends, worthy kinsmen, prosperous and contented life; for a cheerful temper, competence of worldly goods, a fair share of health, interrupted only by such alternations as have taught me the more to value it; for some stock of good reputation; for opportunities of public service, afforded me through the confidence of my fellow townsmen in more than one honorable trust;—and, above all, for a home made dear to me by the affectionate and constant devotion of a wife who has done every thing in her power to render me happy. . . .[1]

At fifty Kennedy still had twenty-five years of his career in business and public affairs before him, but the nostalgic tone of the will was appropriate; nearly all that his contemporaries would most often associate with his name had already been accomplished. Both in literature and politics he had long since won a degree of popular recognition which a fellow Southerner and rival author, William Gilmore Simms, could only envy. In this same year of 1845 Simms dedicated his novel *Count Julian* to Kennedy, noting that the elder writer was "well-known and much admired" for the three works of fiction which he had published in the 1830's, but adding that he had "but too prematurely forborne" to follow them up.[2] Simms, the compulsive professional writer, could not comprehend a man who declined to capitalize on such successes. To Kennedy, however, his literary work was but one element in the full life which he had wished to lead. He was proud of his novels—flattered that his contemporaries thought them a lasting contribution to the small store of native literature—yet there were always other calls upon his time to be heeded, other ambitions to pursue. Lawyer, politician, businessman, author, Cabinet officer, public benefactor—Kennedy reveled in all of these roles. He would be surprised to know that, nearly a century after his death, his countrymen find in three of his books—*Swallow Barn, Horse-Shoe Robinson,* and *Rob of the Bowl*—reason enough to value him.

I *Baltimore Town*

Kennedy was born on October 25, 1795, in the burgeoning seaport town of Baltimore, Maryland.[3] His parentage was a mixed one, and he never quite freed himself from the opposing pulls implicit in his heritage. His father, an emigrant from Ireland, had followed two brothers to seek financial opportunities in the New World; after an early start in Philadelphia, he moved to Baltimore in the 1790's to set up a branch of the family mercantile business. Kennedy's mother, on the other hand, was a Pendleton of Virginia, an offspring of a Tidewater clan which could trace its American origins to the seventeenth century and one which had performed gallantly on the revolutionary side during the War of Independence. Like Simms, who also had an Irish emigrant father and a mother with family roots in Virginia, Kennedy was more conscious of his Southern background than he was of his European blood. Certainly it was his mother, a "fine, majestic-looking woman" who lived until 1854, who was the dominant force in family life. In later years he recalled that she had a "degree of command in her family which very decidedly directed its opinions: and, from her possessing more intellect than my father, he has always quietly yielded to her influence."[4]

Mrs. Kennedy was not fond of Baltimore—especially of the jungle heat of its summers—and for several months yearly she uprooted her growing family (John was the eldest of four sons) for visits with her own people in western Virginia. By Kennedy's own account, life in the country was often a brisk course of rides, hunts, dances, and evening story-telling sessions. It was a secure, self-centered, even smug society that he observed, one proud of its family networks and its institutions—of all that would later be encompassed in that regionally hallowed term "the Southern way of life." Kennedy looked back on these sojourns with mingled affection and amusement; and in his first book, *Swallow Barn,* he strove to preserve his impressions of what this culture had been.

In 1809, after basic schooling in private institutions, Kennedy entered Baltimore College; he completed the course of study in 1812, despite the fact that ready cash had grown scarce after reverses in his father's enterprises. At this recently founded college he gained his first real acquaintance with some of the authors who would be leading influences on his own work: "I studied Greek a whole winter [he wrote later], by rising before daylight—I read Locke, Hume, Robertson—all the Essayists and poets, and many of the metaphysicians . . . made copious notes on all subjects which came within my study . . . read French, Spanish and *began* German—copied large portions of Pope's translation of Homer, and wrote critical notes upon it, as I went along."[5]

Inevitably at this date the major eighteenth-century English essaysists—Addison, Steele, Johnson—were taught to the youth as models of both rhetoric and morality. Yet Kennedy also relished the fiction of Defoe, Goldsmith, and Sterne, whose *Tristram Shandy* and *A Sentimental Journey* were immediate favorites. "I wrote a great many things, in what I thought the same vein—," he once reminisced, "the page filled with dashes, and an imitation of that eccentric transition, and the parenthesis, and the personal conjuration of the reader, which are to be found in all of Sterne's books."[6] The stimulation of his wide reading also set his pen to racing away at other, more ambitious, topics; at the age of eighteen he was forced to remind himself that his enthusiasm had thus far outrun his ability to bring any single topic to proper completion:

> Never was a person more than myself the sport of whim and caprice—lately considering the number of literary enterprises I have in contemplation, I find the following, most of which are at present under my hand—Historical characters—Microcosm—

> Essay on Sympathy—Satire on Criticisms—An oration exemplified —Opinion on works of mind—private memories—Letters—Notes on Blair—Essay on Religion—System of fortification—Portraits of nature—Diversions—Notes on Natural Law—Sentimental Remarks—
>
> About a year ago I burnt a collection I had made, called the Budget, which had swelled to a size sufficient to fill a volume—I'm sorry for having destroyed these, as nothing could give me more pleasure than to revise them.[7]

Kennedy received the bachelor of arts degree from Baltimore College in November, 1812, just five months after the United States had opened the second war against England. Like many other local patriots who were eager to protect Baltimore's vital seafaring interests, he joined the United Volunteers of the Fifth Regiment of Maryland Militia; and in 1814 he participated in the battles of Bladensburg and North Point. Yet the War of 1812, intoxicating as it was to a youth hot for military glory, did not keep him from worrying about a permanent career. During periods when he was not on active duty with his regiment, he halfheartedly studied law in the office of his uncle, Edmund Pendleton; but he also found he could not give up the apprenticeship to literature which had lured him at college.

The chief harvest of Kennedy's late teens was a series of dull essays which bore the title of "The Swiss Traveller." Composed in 1813, they first saw print in a Baltimore monthly magazine, the *Portico,* between February and August, 1816.[8] Kennedy adopted in them the familiar eighteenth-century "foreign traveler" device, in which the author assumed the mask of a visitor from abroad in order to report on the peculiarities of the society around him. The technique had proved amusing in the hands of a Goldsmith or an Irving, but Kennedy had not yet developed the lightness of touch which still gives some life to the *Citizen of the World* or the *Salmagundi* papers. Heavy-handed, redundant, pseudo-Addisonian in their prose rhythms, the "Swiss Traveller" essays quickly weary the modern reader; and they may be quickly dismissed.

Kennedy's protagonist is one Sidney, an emigrant from Switzerland; he is not concerned, though, with the satirical perspective but with panegyric; Sidney is a mere mouthpiece for the author's own praise of a rising America. One passage serves to give the essential flavor of the series. Sidney has been expatiating on the Swiss devotion to personal liberty; now, an exile from a land oppressed by the French, he hopes that America will carry on the tradition:

> Here then, may I hope to see the prosperity, the Roman republicanism that invasion has expelled from Switzerland? . . . I will imagine even if the reality should contradict the fiction, that America is still the abode of heroes and patriots. That the happiness of the republick is still the first and great care of every citizen: that he considers her glory as his birth-right, and the support of it the special charge of those who gave it life. That the youth of the country are instructed by precept how valuable is their constitution, and animated by example to die in its defence. That private interest is despicable and unmanly in competition with publick good. That the sacrifices of affection, fortune and life are not too great for the welfare of the country. That simplicity of manners, contempt for luxury, and honest independent principle, are the safe-guards of their liberty and the assurance of their happiness. . . .[9]

As literature, these essays could interest only the most desperate antiquarian, and the best that can be said for them is that they do vaguely foreshadow both the concern with style and the nationalism of Kennedy's mature work. The formal Neo-Classical rhetoric which he imitated was no longer viable when he wrote; it had become a mere school exercise. But at very least such composition was useful to a novice; and it was a heady experience, he found, to see his words in print under the auspices of a locally distinguished literary society. More importantly, he had now joined ranks with those patriots who were trumpeting that American writers should hew to native subjects and reveal the glories of democracy. His predecessors Irving and Cooper would often move to foreign soil for their subjects, but Kennedy himself never forgot his early commitment.

II *The Red Book*

In the years following the close of the War of 1812, Kennedy rather reluctantly entered his chosen profession of the law. Admitted to the bar in 1816, he was honored by the patronage of eminent elders; but no great press of clients followed him. Legal prolixity and trivial wrangles disheartened the young man; even years later, in *Swallow Barn*, he could not resist a dig at the pretentiousness of his cohorts: "It [a document in a legal row] was filled with discussions upon reversionary interests, resulting uses, and all the jargon of the books, plentifully embellished with a prodigious array of learning, contained in pithy Latin maxims, in which the lawyers are wont to invest meagre and common thoughts with the veil of science."[10]

But financial necessity drove him on, for even established literary men found life difficult without some subsidiary income. And now there was no help to be gained from his family. His father, having failed even to satisfy his business debts, at last quit Baltimore entirely; in 1820 he removed his family, except for his eldest son, to a farm in western Virginia which Mrs. Kennedy had inherited from her father.[11] John, meanwhile, had joined three other fledgling lawyers in maintaining a co-operative bachelor establishment, where all rejoiced in imagining themselves young blades. One of these men, Peter Hoffman Cruse, had—like Kennedy—a stronger passion for urbane literature than for legal briefs; and the two soon began amusing themselves with plans for a side career in belles lettres.

The chief fruit of the Cruse-Kennedy collaboration was ten numbers of an ambitious satirical periodical which they named the *Red Book*. Published through a Baltimore bookseller at various times between 1819 and 1821, the *Red Book* became something of a local success; but it is fatally derivative, and its many topical allusions make much of it meaningless to the modern reader. Modeling their styles and subject matter on eighteenth-century British periodicals like the *Spectator*, the authors fancied they could bring to the Baltimore scene the sophisticated outlook of an Addison or a Steele. Part of their own fun was in disguising themselves behind a number of pseudonyms, and they relished the attempts to penetrate their masks. They proclaimed satire as their chief end; but their evident desire was more to titillate their customers than to "correct" the manners of the town, as can be seen in their first "Advertisement":

> This little book comes before the publick eye, the careless offspring of chance, unsupported by patronage and unadorned by the tinsel of name or fashion. . . . It possesses this advantage, that let the world slight it as it may, it will always be *red*. . . .
>
> It is vain to seek into its origin, for no man shall tell whence it comes. The authors are not to be known, though they mingle freely with their fellows:—their situation protects them from scrutiny and even from suspicion. Many, it is predicted, will become the objects of conjecture, and every man's eye will be turned to some suspicious victim, whose genius will entitle him to the odium of our pen. Imputation will be as unjust, as search will be useless; we beg all to pause before they accuse.
>
> However hidden the *source* of this book, its *destiny* shall not be obscure; we can easily foresee the several vicissitudes it shall encounter in its passage from the press to the toilette—from the toilette to the curls of dance-worn belles and conquest-seeking ladies. We feel but little anxiety or interest in its fate. From our hands it passes rapidly, and is left like Noah's dove, to find its own resting place. To the publick we dare commend it as a friend:—we know what it deserves, and leave it upon the wide world, almost equally reckless of favour or of disappointment.[12]

The various numbers of the *Red Book* are made up of satirical essays and verse, the former largely Kennedy's, the latter Cruse's; it is possible, too, that some friend may occasionally have lent a hand. Cruse, who was to die of cholera in 1832 after helping Kennedy with the publication of *Swallow Barn,* had serious literary hopes; and his stanzas show a thorough absorption of satirical Latin poetry and adaptations of its manner and matter in the Neo-Classical period. This excerpt—from "Horace in Baltimore: To Fashion" in the first number—is a fair sample of his easy prosody and his critical temper:

> Thou speak'st, and maidens soft and bright
>   Each touch of native sweetness banish:
> Thou speak'st, and by thy magick might
>   Deformity and dulness vanish:
> Citherea's zone, the Poets tell,
>   Could beautify the ugliest faces;
> But thine, bright lady, bears the bell,
>   And clothes with worth as well as graces.[13]

Kennedy's prose essays, sketches, and parodies often focused on that antique and usually dreary target: the conduct of women in fashionable society. There were also mock epistles, supposedly composed by an Indian chief, on puzzling doings in "Bawl-ti-more"; there were occasional character sketches and a few travel episodes. Though the authors referred to the wounded cries of their victims, it is not likely that many egos were deflated by the authors' blunted shafts. Indeed, it was something of a compliment to treat the belles of an only relatively sophisticated American town as if they really were the women of the great world they liked to think themselves. If today we find the authors of the *Red Book* relying too heavily on borrowed genres and speaking with a conspicuously "un-American" voice, we should recall that these were literary models which neither they nor the objects of their amusement had yet learned—or dared—to go beyond. In an America which could free herself politically but not culturally from England, there were doubtless many readers who found the imitative tone of the *Red Book* not entirely displeasing. For example, William Wirt, the distinguished lawyer whose biography Kennedy would one day write, commented to a friend who had sent him a copy:

> I am much obliged to you for the Red-Book—which I have read throughout—it is written with great ease and sprightliness, and displays some fine strokes both of conception & execution—the moral being every where I think unimpeachable—with the exception, perhaps, of the attacks upon old maids, whose state, not being a voluntary one, is a misfortune & therefore not lawful game for the satirist—his proper objects are follies and vices—but they ought, perhaps, to be attacked only in the abstract or exhibited perhaps in a *really* fictitious character. . . .[14]

And Edward Everett, editor of the powerful *North American Review,* informed the exuberant Kennedy that he had found much talent in the work.

Early in 1821, however, both authors were beginning to tire of continuing the project indefinitely; Cruse wrote to Kennedy:

> I have come to the conclusion in my own mind, that circumstances will not permit us to finish it until its appearance would be ridiculous from the delay. . . . We have gained all our

> objects in a greater degree than I had anticipated. *I* am content; and as we have signalized the commencement of our friendship by a joint literary labour, I hope and firmly trust we shall ever be allies in thought, principle & action. It is certainly time for us to be doing something better than writing R. Books. . . .[15]

Kennedy, now engrossed in the beginnings of his political career, readily agreed. In March the tenth and last number appeared—after some prodding of Kennedy by Cruse—and the proud young authors formally let their public know who they were.

III *The Lure of Politics*

Kennedy's longing for literary fame always ran behind his attraction to politics and public affairs. Though he was increasingly to be involved with the nationalist-minded mercantile class, he remained something of a Southerner in his conviction that the composition of imaginative literature was the avocation of a gentleman and not a full-time pursuit. In 1820, even while the *Red Book* was still appearing, he won his first elective political post; and for the next three years he served in the Maryland House of Delegates. Attractive in appearance, urbane in manner, forceful and witty in his speech, he was able to serve his constituents well in the state capital. In the years since his birth Baltimore had become a leading trade center of the upper South; manufactured goods poured over its wharves, and its fast clipper ships opened a lucrative intercourse with distant points of the globe. His own family, with businesses in Philadelphia and Baltimore, had early been committed to the full expansion of industry and trade. It is to be expected, then, that Kennedy tended to look to the North rather than to the South for leadership in the country's growth and to see the problems of both regions essentially in economic terms.[16] Slavery, for example, he felt would come naturally to an end when increased competition from free workers made it financially unsound; although he would come to speak of it as a moral evil, he distrusted immediate radical change in property rights; and he had sympathy for the Southerner's fear and hatred of Northern abolitionist agitators.

In the state legislature Kennedy busied himself with projected internal improvements, urging development of local waterways and calling for construction of a Chesapeake-Delaware Canal. His enthusiasm for such schemes brought him his first political setback, in 1823, when the subject of a canal along the Potomac River was introduced. Accepting the nationalist view of an artery which would open up Western markets and benefit the coal industry, he was not prepared for the hostility of Baltimoreans who feared that the citizens of Washington might gain at their expense. As a state Maryland was still torn between the interests of its agricultural counties and its one large city; Kennedy's constituents saw only a betrayal in his vote to subscribe stock in a Potomac canal company. In Baltimore censure of its young representative was demanded, and there were mutterings that he ought to be hanged in effigy. Kennedy, anxious to defend his action and to set forth the implicit worth of the scheme, contributed four closely reasoned articles to the Baltimore *American*, but he failed to carry his point.[17]

Whatever the justice of his stand, he now lost most of the good will which he had carefully built up as a young legislator. His fellow townspeople were further annoyed by the knowledge that he had, in the preceding year, been recommended for a diplomatic post in the new republic of Chile and hence had affairs other than theirs on his mind. The appointment—of the sort which would help to sustain Irving—did come through early in 1823. But by this time Kennedy had cooled in his enthusiasm for a sojourn which would take him away from his law practice and in which he could see no assurance of personal advancement. He therefore declined the honor before the mission left for South America.

At this point, when his political career was temporarily blocked, Kennedy was wed to Mary Tenant, daughter of a wealthy local shipping merchant.[18] But just nine months after the ceremony, which had taken place in January, 1824, Mary died in childbirth; and the baby born to them survived only a while longer. The disconsolate widower first sought another diplomatic post, which was now refused him; and in 1826 he decided to shift to the national scene by running for the House of Representatives. But the electorate had not forgotten the views he had expressed in his last term in the Maryland legislature, and he was badly defeated in the fall voting. There was nothing to do now but return to his law practice and defer for a time his hope for further office.

Late in 1827 Kennedy began courting Elizabeth Gray, daughter of an Irish immigrant whose cotton-spinning mill on the Patapsco River a few miles west of Baltimore had made him well-to-do. Their union in 1829, though it proved childless, was the stabilizing influence throughout Kennedy's many remaining years. His chatty and amusing letters to his wife, preserved among his papers, reveal the depth of his affection for a woman who, if not his intellectual equal, still provided him the home life and security which he had lacked since his own family had moved from the city. With his father-in-law, Edward Gray, who kept a cottage near his business at Ellicott's Mills, Kennedy was always on excellent terms. Their economic views—particularly on the protective tariff—already chimed harmoniously. As recent biographers have pointed out, there is no basis for accepting Parrington's charge that Kennedy altered his opinions under the influence of the "masterful" Gray.[19] In his private journal Kennedy recorded the opinion that his father-in-law was the "tenderest, lovingest, most considerate man,—full of the finest impulses and most generous qualities I have ever found in any."[20]

Gray's impulsive generosity sometimes took the form of cash gifts when the older man was particularly pleased with some political or economic essay by his son-in-law, and there can be no doubt that Kennedy now basked in the financial security his marriage had gained him. Though he continued his profitable law practice until 1840, he devoted more and more of his energies in acting as a recognized spokesman for the business interests of the region. After the young couple built their first home on Baltimore's Mount Vernon Place in 1834, the Grays—father and unmarried daughter—often stayed there; and in the summers the two families trooped off to the cooler air of the Gray establishment by the Patapsco. In such a setting Kennedy could indulge his taste for a comfortable home and his passion for book collecting.

The early years of his marriage passed pleasantly for Kennedy. Though he was often away on business and legal matters in Philadelphia and Washington, he had now settled himself permanently in Baltimore. The town, though less a center of traditional culture than Charleston or Philadelphia, offered its round of lectures, theater, ballet, and music—and such occasional popular attractions as the Siamese twins and an exhibition of Maelzel's "Cathedral of Rheims."[21] The Kennedy house became a nucleus for more intellectual pursuits and offered a pleasant stopping place for visiting celebrities. The Monday Club, which gathered weekly for an evening of good talk, was founded by Kennedy to bring together top-ranking members of the professional and business circles of the city. At times over the next decade he also welcomed to his home visitors like the successful Irving, the struggling Poe, and such distinguished foreigners as Thackeray, Harriet Martineau, and Joseph Bonaparte.

Kennedy's was a patrician circle, but it was not a rigorously closed one. It applauded success in any respectable field of endeavor, but it expected the attributes of a gentleman in those who came to its social gatherings. It was not highly intellectual, though Kennedy and some of his friends did take an active role in the establishment of a state university. Quite as a matter of course it accepted the ownership of real property as the basis for order in a democracy, and it emphasized that the true function of the republic was not to make equal or to level downward but to permit the opportunity for a citizen to rise to the height of his personal capacities. Kennedy's circle was generally optimistic and forward-looking, convinced that the future of a strong America lay in the hands of its business leaders. Kennedy's own youthful experiences quite fitted the pattern: he had been trained as a lawyer, and he had married twice into solid mercantile families. As a lawyer he was by profession a conservator, a guardian of inalienable property rights, one who appealed to established precedent—even though he confessed that the actual processes of the courts were stupid and wearying. The society of merchants and manufacturers—his father-in-law included—he found more stimulating since they both preached the need for progress, in which he believed, and practiced a conservative system of management and labor.

In the estimation of his own circle, Kennedy had now fully "arrived." But his secondary ambition to win recognition as a creative writer was as yet unfulfilled, and there was no better time than this to try his hand. The cultural barrenness of America was a persistent taunt, and there was the continuing danger that absorption in material growth would cause Americans to lose sight of beginnings and eventual goals. There was a strong didactic streak in Kennedy that made him want to address his countrymen directly, to open their eyes while entertaining them. What he chose to do, therefore, in this decade following his second marriage, was to expend at least part of his energies on three long works of fiction—works to be examined in detail in succeeding chapters. But it is appropriate at this point to note that each story involves a segment of the American past; each contributes a bit to the sense of national identity which America so desperately needed; each proclaims the stabilizing and conservative virtues which Kennedy found in the society in which he moved; and each sets in dialectical opposition to this tradition the ideal of progress to which Kennedy had dedicated himself. If his own circle continued to value him more as the man of public affairs, the historian of our literature can be grateful that he occasionally yielded to his other commitments.

IV *Before* Swallow Barn

Before I turn to an analysis of *Swallow Barn*, it will be helpful briefly to review the status of American fiction prior to the decade of the 1830's when Kennedy published all his major books. From early days American colonials had read novels or "romances" imported from abroad, and they had themselves developed minor types like the semifictional narratives of captivity by Indians.[22] But the rise of the native novel—which would prove to be the chief distinction of our literature by the 1850's—was agonizingly slow, and the earliest examples were often embarrassingly puerile.

The first would-be novelists were handicapped by a number of prejudices against the form itself. For one thing, the Puritan contempt for fiction persisted long after Puritanism had waned as a religious force; those influenced by it argued that the novel was baldly indecent, that it held damnable European codes of manners and morals up to admiration, that it encouraged idleness, that it was nonutilitarian. Other critics objected that since it was by definition a "fiction" it projected a false view of life, and it encouraged readers to associate themselves with characters and situations which had no objective reality. Still others condemned it on the grounds that it was not an ancient and Classical mode—and hence not an inherently respectable one.

The pressure of these arguments may be measured by the various defenses which early novelists constantly made of their work. The best response to the charge of immorality was, clearly, to claim the opposite: to insist that the novel actually promoted morality by painting vice as black and virtue as attractive. The author often flaunted the banner of morality in a preface and homilies spotted throughout the text. He was, nonetheless, in a quandary: scenes of sexual titillation and not appeals to chaste behavior sold books. The writer therefore often went as far as he could in detailing the events of a seduction and then cooled the reader off with a fine spray of piety. Such was the strategy which can be observed in what is generally accepted as the first authentically American novel, William Hill Brown's *The Power of Sympathy,* published in Boston in 1789. It is also characteristic of one of the most popular books ever written in America, Susanna Rowson's *Charlotte Temple* (1794); and its influence extended far into the nineteenth century. Kennedy himself never condescended to such suggestiveness, but he was unable to jettison the central love story which was supposed to be a necessary lure for feminine readers.

A second major criticism—that novels were false in their presentation of reality, that they lied about life—also brought a corresponding response. Writers claimed that their stories were "founded in truth" or were "based on fact." They averred that they had documents to support the accuracy of their tales, and they frequently adopted the pose that they were merely the recorders and not the inventors of the action. Thus Kennedy asserts in *Swallow Barn* that his sketch of life in Virginia is faithfully copied from direct observation; he proclaims the historicity of the background events in *Horse-Shoe Robinson* and *Rob of the Bowl.* Like other writers of the period, he was still somewhat on the defensive; he was uneasily aware that a faint aura of brimstone clung to the writer of a novel—and even to its reader.

But, in spite of all attempts to suppress them, native authors had contrived by the opening decades of the nineteenth century to produce several classes of fiction and to win a steadily expanding audience. Because of a cultural lag, because of a pragmatic desire to imitate proven products of the homeland, and because of a lack of original geniuses at the outset, earlier works of fiction written in America were highly derivative—and usually as badly written as their outraged critics claimed them to be. Kennedy, an avid reader of both the foreign and the home-grown product, would have been aware of four major types of fiction; these were the sentimental, the Gothic, the satirical-picaresque, and the historical. The Gothic, which demanded special stage sets, never really caught on in America, though its darkly melodramatic villains would long stalk the native scene; the satirical-picaresque, perhaps too "intellectual" for the average taste, had a local success only in Hugh Henry Brackenridge's *Modern Chivalry,* which appeared in stages between 1792 and 1815. But the sentimental-didactic, deriving largely from Samuel Richardson's *Pamela,* flourished to excess. American imitators of Richardson off-handedly stole from him such devices as the epistolary framework, the virtuous heroine in sequential distress, the charming but corrupted seducer. Other domestic novelists, less daring, took as a model Oliver Goldsmith's *The Vicar of Wakefield* and drenched their audiences with tearful-cheerful views of ordinary home life.

Yet it was the historical romance which would prove to be the form most widely copied by American writers. Events like the Revolution and Indian warfare had already provided subjects for some of the earliest novelists, but the real vogue began only after the success of Sir Walter Scott's *Waverley* (1814) and James Fenimore Cooper's *The Spy* (1821). Cooper was without question the most significant writer of fiction in America during the decade of the 1820's. His discovery of the usable materials of national history and his intuitive perception of a haunting theme in the clashes of frontier life gave to his stories an interest which still persists, despite their irritating technical flaws; and his practice was a model which other writers like Simms and Kennedy gratefully accepted.

One other American writer was ranked alongside Cooper in this endeavor to create a national literature, though he never produced any long works of fiction. He was, of course, Washington Irving, whose *Sketch Book* (1819-20) at once appealed to readers on both sides of the Atlantic. Irving had discovered—in effect, invented—the Dutch colonial period in his *Knickerbocker's History of New York* (1809) and in such later short tales as "Rip Van Winkle" and "The Legend of Sleepy Hollow." His urbane prose style, his wit, and his gentle sentimentality were unmatched in America during the early years of his career; and his works appeared to Kennedy and many of his contemporaries sufficient retorts to European sneers at our cultural rawness. Kennedy would one day become a personal friend of Irving, but his debt was always to the *Sketch Book* and *Bracebridge Hall* and not to any direct influence of the man.

In sum, then, the reading of Kennedy's early years would have provided for him both inescapable models and basic assumptions about the creation of fiction. Certainly, a balanced and "correct" style was a prerequisite, grounded as he was in the eighteenth-century essayists and in the books of Irving. He would have agreed, too, with his predecessors that fiction properly inculcated moral lessons as well as provided entertainment. These lessons, as Irving and Cooper had demonstrated, were to be sought in the American past; early a nationalist in politics, Kennedy found it easy to accept an America-first program for literature. This view would lead him, as it had led Cooper, to seek out story materials in those areas with which he had been acquainted since childhood—Virginia and Maryland. He would never go farther afield.

It is important to understand at the outset that Kennedy, though he concurred with Cooper in holding that the writer of fiction should not consciously misrepresent the actual deeds of history, was no "realist" in any modern sense of that term; he could freely invent characters and plots, so long as he remained faithful to what he considered to be the inner truth of events. Kennedy was, above all, concerned with helping to fabricate for America what this country so notoriously lacked—a vision of the unique experiences which it had undergone, a sense of its own special identity. In short, he supported the sort of reinterpretation which the imaginative artist and not the professional historian could best supply. Kennedy would create no large-scale "myth" for America, as Simms did for his own region of the lower South;[23] when he became absorbed in public affairs, he declined the effort of further publication. But during the decade of the 1830's, at least, his duty was clear to him. Convinced after his experience with the *Red Book* that he had a genuine talent, he now turned to more creative art with the hope that he might exhibit those virtues which the American past had developed—and which should be conserved in the present as a foundation upon which to build the future.

CHAPTER 2

Swallow Barn: The Double Focus

I *The Search for Form*

WITH HIS FINANCIAL SITUATION relatively secure and his political ambitions temporarily frustrated, Kennedy found time late in 1829 to shift his attention to his creative writing. As his journal entries and other manuscript materials reveal, he had for some time contemplated composing a volume of sketches of the Virginia country life which he had known from boyhood.[1] Keeping an eye on Irving's recent successes with the *Sketch Book* and *Bracebridge Hall,* Kennedy initially had thought of making an observer-narrator of a young painter—a "picturesque traveler" who, like Irving's Geoffrey Crayon, would record whatever struck his fancy during his random wanderings. In a manuscript chapter which dates from the early stages of this scheme, Kennedy has his artist begin the action by arriving at a hotel in Richmond as he makes his way toward "the western parts of Virginia":

> I was provided [the narrator tells us] with a small portfolio, [some Bristol boards,] and a good collection of crayons. Moreover, I had procured a neat little vehicle somewhat of the wagon shape with a kind of gig-body in the middle, leaving space enough behind to carry a convenient supply of baggage and a light fowling piece: to this belonged a sturdy pony with a slouch look and a very thorough-going, resolute gait. Thus equipped as a picturesque buccaneer I was ready to set forward on my voyage to whatever seas promised the best booty.[2]

But at the Richmond hotel the narrator runs into a young Virginian named Hazard, whom he had once met in New York; and Hazard persuades him to postpone his mountain junket in favor of a visit to a Tidewater plantation, Hoppergallop House, presided over by his brother-in-law, Frank Oldstock. A succeeding draft passage, later reworked into Chapter I of *Swallow Barn,* describes in detail this "low-browed, aristocratical old castle that squats like a brooding hen on the Northern Bank of the Rappahannock, not far from the confluence of that river with the Chesapeake." From these pages and other working notes it can be concluded that Kennedy's over-all design was to continue with an extended satirical portrait of the way of life of Oldstock, who is an archetypal Virginia planter proud of his family and state, arrogant of manner, and short of cash.

Some years later, Kennedy recalled this first intention and his second thoughts in a letter to the publisher of a new edition of *Swallow Barn:* "The original idea of Swallow Barn was connected with a plan to write a kind of Headlong Hall story—rather of the comic and satirical kind. I meant to represent an old decayed place with odd and crochetty people inhabiting it—and with that purpose took the present name. The plan was changed afterwards, but the name retained without proper consideration or attention to it until the book was printed:—too late to correct it. So, I never liked it afterwards."[3]

Scattered entries in Kennedy's journal also record stages in this change of plan. As he completed segments of his story, he showed them to friends for their reaction and criticism. On October 13, 1829, he made this note: "Mitchell suggested to me an alteration in my plan of 'Swallow Barn' which I shall follow. It is to drop the young painter and give it without introduction." And a few days later he wrote, "On Saturday [October 17] I commenced my Swallow Barn on the new plan, and finished the first chapter." Though he permanently jettisoned the young painter, he wished to keep the frame story device of the foreign traveler who comes to observe Virginia; his chief technical problem now was how to account for his narrator's keeping such detailed notes. His solution was hardly an original one. Mark, the narrator, would pen a long letter to a friend back in New York State describing his arrival and adding a series of informal sketches showing "the condition and peculiarities of Swallow Barn" as he first saw it. The friend was to respond eagerly, and Mark would promise to keep a journal which would be sent at intervals. A rather static opening, then, could be relieved by succeeding chapters building up some narrative suspense.[4]

Kennedy now pressed ahead, and within a month he had completed the first five chapters by writing for an hour in the afternoon and for a part of each evening. A simultaneous project was the compilation of a long memoir of Captain John Smith, which he hoped to work somewhere into the text; though excised from later editions, it was to occupy thirty-five pages of the original version.[5] Journal entries over the next few months register his feeling he was "getting on fast" with the book. For some months after February, 1830, there was a hiatus in composition; but in September of that year he noted that he had recently taken up *Swallow Barn* again for the "purpose of writing out the last impression for the press." He added, "I have changed the name of Oldstock to Meriwether at [Peter Hoffman] Cruse's suggestion."

This dropping of a mere label for the owner of the plantation hints that Kennedy continued to alter his concept of his materials during the process of composition; and the supposition is borne out by a journal entry of January 30, 1831: "I finished the first volume of Swallow Barn on Sunday the 16th inst. I began to write it on the 21st of September last and the greater part is entire new matter." This new matter was, of course, the chapters which add a running story or plot complication to the initial series of sketches. Kennedy's work on the book continued at intervals throughout 1831, for he remarked on November 19: "Ever since my return from Virginia until about the 20th of October I was steadily engaged on the second volume of Swallow Barn." And then, laconically, he recorded on the last day of 1831: "Finished Swallow Barn."

As finally completed, *Swallow Barn* differed considerably from Kennedy's first concept, but it still showed indebtedness to the method of Irving. The narrator, Mark Littleton, no longer is a random traveler; he is a New Yorker who has been invited by his Virginia cousin, Ned Hazard, to spend some summer months at Swallow Barn, an old plantation on the James River not far from Richmond. The book now begins with an "Introductory Epistle" from Littleton to a fellow New Yorker, Zachary Huddlestone, in which he explains the circumstances of his visit and promises to keep him informed of amusing happenings in the Old Dominion. This frame story is maintained for a while in somewhat desultory fashion; but, except as it attempts to reflect the view of an outsider concerning Virginian manners, it is never very important. For the sketches of the inhabitants of Swallow Barn soon suggest minor plot lines (which will be discussed later), and the book for a time assumes the pace of a conventional novel. The main influences on these departures from the model of Irving are patently those of Laurence Sterne in the digressions and descriptions of the actions of quixotic individuals; Tobias Smollett and Henry Fielding in the handling of inset narratives and in the treatment of country squires; and Thomas Love Peacock in the country-house setting. Moreover, the construction of the main love plot and the dialogue of the young ladies is clearly an echo of the eighteenth-century comedy of manners, particularly the plays of Richard Brinsley Sheridan and Oliver Goldsmith.

Perhaps Kennedy reasoned that such additions would make his book generally more popular than a parochial satirical dissection of Virginia would have been. But he was now at least certain that it was a salable text; and on February 2, 1832, he noted in his journal that his old friend Cruse had been assigned to offer the manuscript to Carey & Lea, the well-known Philadelphia publishing house. Cruse's jockeying with Henry C. Carey, senior partner of the firm which published Irving and Cooper, attests to the poor bargaining position of the unknown author of the period. Carey liked the idea of the book, but he was cagey in his promises, at first offering a few hundred dollars for outright purchase of the copyright.[6] Cruse, however, pressed for a better arrangement for the author; and, after his return to Baltimore in late February, Kennedy recorded this proposal for publication:

> That Carey should publish at his own expense and out of the proceeds of the sale of the 1st Edition to give me what mutual friends upon an exhibition of all the accounts should say I ought to have. Carey told Cruse that no new author, not even Wash-

ington Irving nor Cooper had rec[eived] any thing in this country upon their first works: That it would not be safe to venture upon a larger edition than one thousand copies to try the market. If it succeeded the subsequent editions might become valuable. . . . As soon as Cruse got home (on the 22nd) he rec[eived] a letter from Carey telling him that having read some of the first chapters he was very much pleased, and would be willing to give $500 for the copy right.

At Kennedy's request, Cruse refused any outright sale and accepted the alternative proposition. On February 29 Carey wrote directly to Kennedy to say that his wife had liked what she had thus far read; and, apparently referring to Kennedy's tolerant attitudes toward some Southern institutions mentioned in the story, he added: "If it should produce such a feeling as you desire you will have rendered a great service to the nation—Each portion of the Union looks with a feeling of dislike towards the other, when it requires only to know them better to see admirable qualities in every portion—The Yankee dislikes the Virginian & the Virginian despises the Yankee, when a stranger would find good reason to admire both—" More enthusiastic now, Carey acknowledged that the author had done well to refuse the $500 offer since Carey & Lea had decided to print two thousand copies and there was promise of excellent profits.

During the next few months, both in Philadelphia and in Baltimore, Kennedy attended to the details of seeing *Swallow Barn* through the press. Issued in two neat volumes, released within a few weeks of each other in the spring of 1832, the book quickly caught on with the public; and a guessing game began as to the identity of the "Mark Littleton" who had signed the dedication and the preface. Since several of Kennedy's friends had seen the work in its manuscript stages, gossip soon got around that he was its progenitor; and once again he basked in the pleasant light of local fame.

Throughout the late spring and summer, Carey continued to send Kennedy encouraging bulletins; and, with an eye to future business, he observed that the reception of the book so far would "warrant you in going on with your second." By mid-June Carey reported that 1,250 copies had been sent out; and he inflated Kennedy's ego further by quoting a "literary gentleman" who had said that the book was "better than any thing Cooper or Irving had written." In New York, James Kirke Paulding, the well-known author and influential critic, published a flattering notice; and in a letter to Carey, which Carey sent on to Kennedy, he hailed the Americanism of the book: "I feel much interest in the success of this work . . . and earnestly hope the public will receive it in such a manner as to encourage the author to continue his efforts. The time is not far distant when the records of literature in this country will be equal to those of any other in the world, if I don't deceive myself."

In July Kennedy and his wife decamped from Baltimore to escape a bad outbreak of cholera; when they returned in October, he found to his lasting grief that Cruse, his closest literary associate since the old *Red Book* days, had fallen a victim to the disease just a month earlier. Carey, ever the bookseller, reported in a not very felicitous phrase that *Swallow Barn* had been doing very well until the cholera "killed all business." But by December Carey was able to announce that about 1,400 copies had been sold—a splendid record, he thought, for a first book. And in the same month Kennedy wrote to his wife from Philadelphia: "Do you know they make a great parade here about Swallow Barn; and every body who is introduced to me forthwith begins to talk of Ned Hazard, Mike Brown, &c."[7] The year which had begun nervously with the initial dickerings with Carey & Lea had turned out extraordinarily well for all but the unlucky Cruse, who died before his own literary dreams were fulfilled.

II *Verdicts*

Almost all of the early reviewers of *Swallow Barn* found the same things to say about Kennedy's first book. Above all, it reminded them of Irving—especially of his *Sketch Book* and *Bracebridge Hall*—though most were disposed to grant that the model was a worthy one to choose. Second, the "fidelity" of the story to actual life in Virginia was commended, and its humor and its clarity of style were extolled. And, finally, many congratulated themselves on their discovery that another American author had proved the native scene was not entirely devoid of literary interest.

In the scrapbook which he kept for newspaper clippings, Kennedy pasted nearly forty reviews which appeared in American and English periodicals within a short time after publication of the book—a remarkable amount of attention for a fledgling author to attract.[8] Because a notice in the Baltimore *American* is typical of these initial reactions, it warrants quoting at some length:

> *Swallow Barn* does not profess to belong to the class of novels, although it has some pretensions to that title. It has more the character of the *Sketch Book* of Irving. . . . [The author] has produced a book which . . . is highly creditable to himself, and a valuable addition to American Literature. . . .
>
> The merits of *Swallow Barn* consist in the accuracy and beauty of its descriptive writing, the fidelity to nature and individuality of the few characters introduced, the happy facility with which peculiar traits of manners are seized and sketched off, and the tone of healthful and moral feeling which pervades the whole work. There is, moreover, a vein of genuine humor running throughout. . . . We have been so long accustomed, in taking up novels for perusal, to expect as a matter of course, scenes and characters beyond and above what we have ever seen or met with in real life,—passions displayed in their extremes of excitement, and plots involved in mystery and developed by devices no less mysterious,—that we are glad to meet with a book of fiction, in which there is no villain given over hopelessly to the service of sin, no faultless monster to dismay us with the contemplation of unattainable perfections, and none of the desperate encounters, intricate intrigues and diabolical inventions with which novels usually abound. Such offenses against good taste frequently occur among the novel writers of our own country, some of whom have borrowed the worst tone of the worst specimens of the English novel. . . . We welcome therefore with great satisfaction an author whose taste has rejected these vicious and dangerous excesses; and who has confined himself to a portraiture of the amiable and natural, the domestic and cheerful, to characters which we recognize as familiar and consistent, to manners such as we know them to be, and above all, to the scenery and customs of our own country.

The Frederick (Maryland) *Examiner,* happy about Kennedy's preference for a Southern setting, observed: "The Old Dominion, within whose borders the scenes of the novel in question are laid, could furnish many a tale out of which the fertile fancy of a true novelist might weave a glorious romance. . . . There are more Coopers in America than the author of the 'Pilot.'" Other commentators, though convinced of some similarity to various works of Irving, professed uncertainty about the literary class to which *Swallow Barn* belonged. It was not quite a novel of any type with which they were familiar nor yet a romance in the vein of Cooper's American tales; as a writer of a letter to the New York *Commercial Advertiser* mused, it was "neither a novel, nor a romance, nor a history—and yet it smacks somewhat of all three."

English critics, whose slashing censure and condescending tone American writers had cause to dread, were comfortingly mild. The London *Monthly Magazine* found that *Swallow Barn* "affords us an insight into country manners and customs in America with which we were, heretofore, but imperfectly acquainted. . . . Certain it is, there are descriptions here which fall very little short of those so much admired in the works of our own popular novelists, and which far excel the common run of the same species of writing afforded to us by the generality of fiction-mongers. We cordially recommend Swallow Barn to our readers."

But if England's august judges voted favorably, some New England critics were much cooler toward the book. The *North American Review* admitted to some merits, but the critic was neither excited nor very much amused. The Southern way of life —especially its "peculiar institution" of slavery—was a subject fit only for satire in the opinion of the reviewer for the *New England Magazine*. The gentlemen who pass languidly through the story, he wrote,

> are the most ordinary, trifling, useless generation the world ever saw. To be sure, they are kind, hospitable, liberal, and honorable, but how are their lives passed? If this work be what it pretends, a Virginian of condition has no use for his time but to pay and receive visits, to attend courts, and to watch the multiplication of his horses and negroes. These may be very proper employments, and may conduce to the prosperity of the state, but deliver us from such a life. . . . Such lives as the whites lead, may be very satisfactory to themselves, but they are very insipid to the observer. The whole book is a picture of the stillest of still life.[9]

Private reaction to *Swallow Barn* was also occasionally sour. Kennedy had dedicated his book to his lawyer friend William Wirt, who was also renowned as the author of *Letters of the British Spy.* Wirt—who may have recognized traces of himself in the book's similarly named lawyer, Philly Wart—thanked Kennedy in a gracefully phrased note for the "well-turned dedication," though he confessed that he had so far read little of the story itself.[10] But in a letter to another friend, written the same day, Wirt permitted himself a sneering tone: "Pray have you seen a new work called 'Swallow Barn' which is dedicated *to me.* . . . It is a *sort* of novel, of which the scene is laid in Virginia—but it is a *non descript* sort of a novel—very little incident—& a great deal of what is called sketches of characters—."[11] Irving, to whom Kennedy had also sent a copy and in whose response he was edgily interested, wrote a rather noncommittal letter of acknowledgment.[12]

But Cooper, the other best-seller of Carey & Lea's publishing house, was a much more gratifying reader. Carey, pointing out that *Swallow Barn* could not be copyrighted in England because of its prior publication in America (it was in fact pirated there), had asked both Cooper and Irving to try to influence Richard Bentley, their own London publisher, to publish Kennedy's next book. Carey, ever on the outlook for his business interests, was careful to send on to Kennedy a copy of Cooper's reply, in which he promised to do what he could:

> The moment I got your letter, I sat down & read Swallow Barn. We all think it a very clever work & the author a man of merit. Its faults are affectations of style & a want of interest, of which there is enough, however, to make us wish it had more, handled in the same clever manner. The writer has too great a command of language to abuse himself with hard words. Style should be, like the dress of a handsome woman, felt, but not perceived & Mr. Kennedy has too much matter to attend to his manner, beyond the point that is necessary to illustrate the first. Au reste, it is unquestionably the work of one of our ablest men; & if a young man he may aspire to a wide reputation—[13]

In pondering these reviews and personal comments, Kennedy could be assured of at least one fact: his readers believed he had uncovered usable literary materials in the as yet unexplored region of the upper South. He had had only one predecessor worth recalling—George Tucker, whose pioneer Virginia novel, *The Valley of Shenandoah* (1824), was a melodramatic tale leavened with some directly observed detail. In Charleston, Simms had yet to make his full discovery of the vast resources for fiction to be found in the Southern scene. But, unexpectedly, Kennedy did not follow up his success. I can only conjecture that he never wrote a sequel because he had gradually become aware of his own conflicting attitudes toward the Virginia society which he had wished to portray.

There is uneasiness, at any rate, in his own remarks to his readers. In the prefaces to the first edition and a later revised version, he adopted the diffident pose of the amateur writer who had found amusement in setting down his artless impressions and who had no purpose beyond offering entertainment. The book, so Mark Littleton confesses in the original preface, "has ended in a vein altogether different from that in which it set out. There is a rivulet of story wandering through a broad meadow of episode. Or, I might truly say, it is a book of episodes, with an occasional digression into the plot." And the 1851 "Word from the Author to the Reader" advises again that *Swallow Barn* is "not a novel. . . . It was begun on the plan of a series of detached sketches linked together by the hooks and eyes of a traveller's notes. . . . It is, therefore, utterly unartistic in plot and structure, and may be described as variously and interchangeably partaking of the complexion of a book of travels, a diary, a collection of letters, a drama, and a history. . . ."[14] Partly, such comments are traditional gambits for forestalling readers' criticisms; partly, they reflect the expected attitude of the Southern gentleman toward works of "light literature." In either case, they are disingenuous.

For the fact is that *Swallow Barn* underwent several changes of plan designed to make it a more coherent whole; moreover, the final draft was carefully revised by a writer who was vain about correctness of style and varied literary effects. What Kennedy actually is trying to excuse is that his book throughout is at cross-purposes in the treatment of its subject matter, that underneath the surface of a story which is often celebratory of recent Virginia life and the state's past greatness there runs a disturbing counter-current of seriously intended satire. This very ambivalence, however, gives *Swallow Barn* the peculiar interest which the reader today finds in it.

III *Virginia Through Bifocals*

From the date of its original publication to the present, critics of *Swallow Barn* have commended its "fidelity" or the "realism" of its representation of the Old Virginia scene. Its earliest readers, including some of those already referred to, were struck by the verisimilitude of the book; and they reasonably assumed that the characters and events must have been drawn directly from personal observation. In our own period, Kennedy's biographer, Charles H. Bohner—while recognizing that *Swallow Barn* is the prototype of the Southern "plantation legend" in fiction—can still term it "an authentic document in the social history of the South." William S. Osborne, though he reads much of the book as a deliberate burlesque of Irving's *Bracebridge Hall,* also concludes that it is a "close portrait" of Southern ways. And Jay B. Hubbell, the foremost scholar of earlier writing in the South, appraises the book as "the best picture of Virginia life in the early nineteenth century."[15]

Nonetheless, to speak unqualifiedly of the value of *Swallow Barn* as authentic social record is to mislead the present-day reader. The original critics, writing before Realism had been defined as a literary mode, meant primarily that the book was not a "romance"—that, as a commentator cited earlier indicated, its "scenes and characters" did not go "beyond and above what we have ever seen or met with in real life." In short, *Swallow Barn* stuck to the plausible and did not rely on mysterious doings, incredible plot twists, or a diabolical villain for reader interest. Some twentieth-century critics, however, have been less precise. Perhaps because of their own preference for Realism over Romanticism they have tried to "save" some of our earlier works by claiming them as examples of a sort of proto-Realism. But such a rescue operation can only fail with *Swallow Barn.* For its method is *not* closely reportorial; it is *not* an objective rendering of an observed scene. In fact, its techniques are derived from a wide range of stock devices, and its flavor everywhere is "literary." This is not to say that Kennedy did not draw details from his own memories of Virginia; it is to emphasize that he could not decide whether the "true" Virginia was to be sought in the ideal or in the actual. The book is *both* myth and countermyth, and what is most significantly "real" is its revelation of Kennedy's own dilemma in trying to apprehend reality.

In order to see this problem in specific detail, it is necessary first to analyze the narrative content of *Swallow Barn.* Kennedy began it with the vague idea of sending a traveler—a painter—into the mountain regions of Virginia to record whatever amused him. Later this figure was metamorphosed into Mark Littleton, the New Yorker who is invited by his Virginia cousin, Ned Hazard, to spend a summer vacation on the plantation. The frame story device thus became simply a variation on the foreign visitor genre which Kennedy had already experimented with in the early "Swiss Traveller" and *Red Book* sketches. Visitors traditionally tell their story through letters, and so the book begins with an expository epistle in which the self-styled "picturesque tourist" describes his "voyage of discovery" up the James River, past Jamestown, to Richmond and then his overland trek back along the river to Swallow Barn itself. The epistle ends with his welcome to the house by Frank Meriwether, who has married Ned Hazard's sister and is currently master of the estate. Chapter I, a revised version of the "Hoppergallop House" sketch, now sets the scene with a generalized picture of the house and grounds. The mansion is "aristocratical" and "time-honored" (it is "more than a century old"); from it an "extensive tract of land" extends along the river. The eye observing this scene is not that of the careful reporter of the details of an actual place; it is still that of the painter, composing large elements into a harmonious picture: "Some sparse portions of forest vary the landscape, which, for the most part, exhibits a succession of fields clothed with Indian corn, some small patches of cotton or tobacco plants, with the usual varieties of stubble and fallow grounds."[16]

Chapters II through VII, drawn from the model of Irving and the traditional genre of the character sketch, introduce Meriwether, the spokesman for conservatism and anti-nationalism, and the members of his household. The chapter titles in themselves suggest that Kennedy is leaning more on literary models than on direct observation. Meriwether is "A Country Gentleman"; "Family Portraits" presents Meriwether's wife, Lucretia; their son, Rip, "a shrewd, mischievous imp"; and the housekeeper, Mrs. Barbara Winkle (39-43). "Family Paragons" brings on stage the Meriwethers' teen-age daughters, Lucy and Victorine, and Meriwether's only sister, Prudence. This lady is the conventional old maid; devoted to religious societies and the cause of temperance, she is also a confirmed romantic: in her boudoir "may be found exquisite sketches from her pencil, of forms of love and beauty, belted and buckled knights, old castles and pensive ladies, Madonnas and cloistered nuns,—the offspring of an artistic imagination heated with romance and devotion" (48).

Ned Hazard, who appears next, combines elements of literary stereotypes with some facets of Kennedy's own personality. Ned, who is about thirty-three, is gay, spontaneous, frank and occasionally wild—in short, he is a Young Cavalier: "He has slang for the stable-boys, proverbs for the old folks, and a most oratorical overflow of patriotism for the politicians" (52). In earlier years (like Kennedy himself) he had been "seized with a romantic fever which manifested itself chiefly in a conceit to visit South America, and play knight-errant in the quarrel of the Patriots." But, after a disillusioning firsthand look at the patriotic cause, he had returned home "the most disquixotted cavalier that ever hung up his shield at the end of a scurvy crusade" (52-53). The chapter is padded out with an account of Hazard's education at an academy and at Princeton, from which he was expelled for his role in a duel; the more prosaic passages of this account are doubtless drawn from Kennedy's own school days in Baltimore. The discussion of Ned's education leads naturally into the next sketch, one of Mr. Chub, master of the small neighborhood schoolhouse located on the grounds of the Swallow Barn estate. Mr. Chub—parson, philosopher, and book-lover—is partly a reminiscence of Kennedy's teacher at Baltimore College, William Sinclair, but the portrait is still largely a bookish one.[17]

Chapter VII, another passage of commentary rather than action, is called "Traces of the Feudal System"; in it Kennedy expounds the myth of an early "Cavalier" Virginia and then allows Frank Meriwether to speak at length for the present way of life of the gentry class. There are several crucial passages in this chapter, to which I will return in a moment. At this point, Kennedy begins to extend his perspective and to insinuate narrative interest into his rather static series of portraits. Chapter VIII, which concludes the first section of *Swallow Barn,* informs us that about four miles down river lies another old plantation, The Brakes. In his delineation of its proprietor, Isaac Tracy, Kennedy once again fuses a literary stereotype with some local and historical detail:

> The old gentleman was a stark royalist in the days of the Revolution, and only contrived to escape the confiscation of his estate by preserving a strict and cautious neutrality during the war. He still adheres to the ancient costume, and is now observed taking his rides in the morning, in a long-waisted coat, of a snuff color, and having three large figured gilt buttons set upon the cuffs, which are slashed after an antiquated fashion. . . . (77)

Old Mr. Tracy, ever the Tory and the formalist in his manner, has three children: Catharine, an incipient old maid; Bel, "headlong and thoughtless," who will be the heroine of the succeeding action; and Ralph, a dull outdoor type. With this suggestion of the possibilities for plot development offered by the contrasting establishments of Swallow Barn and The Brakes, Kennedy abruptly returns to the frame story (which the reader has almost forgotten) at the beginning of Chapter IX, called "An Eclogue." Littleton tells his correspondent, Zack, that thus far he has entertained him "with a set of pictures from still life"—"a little gallery of landscapes and portraits, which, in my judgment, were necessary as preliminaries to what I may write in future." Further, Littleton informs Zack: "You now understand exactly where I am, and what kind of good people I have around me, and will be all the better prepared for the little romance of domestic life which I am about to weave out of my every-day occurrences. What my romance will come to, it is impossible to foretell, as it is to grow up out of the events of the day" (80).

This ninth chapter now undertakes to evolve the first of the two plot lines which gave a narrative backbone to *Swallow Barn.* Ned Hazard, it develops, has long been in love with Bel Tracy but has been rejected by her. Ned's comically inept wooing is the topic of a good portion of the succeeding chapters, but the courtship is left unresolved until after Littleton's visit has been concluded. Both Bel and Ned are amusingly drawn, and the dialogue between the couple is decidedly superior to passages of the sort in the work of Kennedy's contemporaries. His model here is that staple of the comedy of manners, the headstrong but romantic girl who demands of her lover that she be courted according to her bookish notions of a proper suit. Ned tries to humor her, and even performs such mock-heroic tasks as recapturing Bel's escaped pet hawk; but he continually slips into some manly excess—like fist-fighting—or into some gaucherie which offends Bel's refined taste. Thematically, there is a dash of satire of Southern chivalry in the scenes between Bel and the down-to-earth Ned; but, more practically, the love story is a sop to the female audience which Kennedy hoped to attract.

In Chapter X, which follows upon that in which the love interest is introduced, Kennedy begins unravelling the second of his narrative lines. This action, which occupies the central third of the book (chapters X–XXVII), involves an old disagreement between the Tracy and the Hazard families over some worthless swamp property, which lies along the boundary between The Brakes and Swallow Barn. The serious element here is Kennedy's mockery of litigation, lawyers, and the Virginian's inordinate pride in his personal honor; but the story is developed lightly, with a considerable debt to Sterne's *Tristram Shandy.* As Littleton explains in a historical disgression, his granduncle, Edward Hazard, had in the middle of the eighteenth century decided to erect a flour mill on Apple-pie Branch, the small stream which marks the dividing line between the two estates. To find sufficient ground for the expected mill pond, old Mr. Hazard had arranged with Gilbert Tracy to transfer from The Brakes whatever land would be "found useful and necessary to occupy in the accomplishment of the said design" (142). But the project had ended in an embarrassing failure; the stream was too small to provide water power for more than a short time each day, and the mill building was allowed to fall into ruin.

Littleton's granduncle—a quirky old gentleman who recalls Uncle Toby in *Tristram Shandy*—had then served in the Revolution; but the Tracys, though loyalist to the core, remained neutral in public. By 1790 Swallow Barn had passed to Walter Hazard, Littleton's uncle; The Brakes was in the possession of Isaac Tracy. When Hazard decided to drain the old millpond marsh, he was confounded to discover that Tracy maintained that the area in question rightfully belonged to The Brakes; Tracy was concerned not about the land itself, which was valueless, but about the whole principle of inherited property, which family honor required him to maintain. Litigation ensued, with the courts deciding always in favor of Hazard's claim. Now Frank Meriwether, as the present proprietor of Swallow Barn, had decided to close the dispute by employing two lawyers to arbitrate the question, his plan being to relinquish all rights to the land without further outraging Tracy's concept of justice in the case.

The two lawyers chosen, Singleton Oglethorpe Swansdown and Philpot Wart, are introduced through extended character sketches. Swansdown, a traditional fop, has traveled in Europe, is fussy in his dress, and has literary pretensions; he is the author of a published narrative poem entitled "The Romaunt of Dryasdale." He is the chief butt of the humor in the lawsuit episode, and he supplies further comedy by becoming romantically involved with both Prudence Meriwether and Catharine Tracy; though it is possible that Kennedy had observed his prototype, Swansdown strikes one as essentially a stock figure. Philly Wart, on the other hand, is drawn with more originality; presumably his personality owes something to William Wirt and the country barristers of Maryland and Virginia whom Kennedy had met through his own legal practice. Thoroughly experienced in the peculiarities of Virginia law, and a pragmatist in his manipulation of country juries, Wart is presented both satirically and affectionately. It is Wart who undertakes, at Meriwether's urging, to maneuver the arbitration so that Tracy can be awarded full possession of the contested land; his tactic is to hear the case before all the parties concerned right in the midst of the swamp. The weight of law is clearly on the side of the Swallow Barn faction, but with mock gravity of demeanor Wart contrives to obfuscate the issues while finding for Tracy. This action, which occurs in Chapter XXVII, is a skillful parody of legal forms and a pointed mockery of the judicial process. But the fun could not be indefinitely continued. With the conclusion of the case, Kennedy soon drops both Wart and the plot line involving the mill land, except for occasionally wistful references by old Tracy, who has lost the hobby which gave zest to his life.

Kennedy now had nearly half of the book to go (he had planned it in the expected two volumes), and he must have been in some puzzlement as to how to progress. Portions of the remaining twenty-two chapters continue with the Bel Tracy-Ned Hazard love contest, but Kennedy's solution was to add to his sketches of the Swallow Barn neighborhood while inserting narrative digressions that are in form really short stories. The best of these latter insets is the yarn told by Hafen Blok, a Hessian by birth, a former soldier, and now a poor white who regales the neighborhood with old ballads and folk tales.[18] Hafen narrates the history of one Mike Brown—a hard-drinking, ne'er-do-well blacksmith who is said to have lived in the region—and his encounters with the devil; the plot, which relies on the old "moonraker" anecdote and other folk motifs, is perhaps derived from the oral story-telling sessions in which Kennedy had often taken part during visits to Virginia.

Other episodes in this last section of the book involve a possum hunt, a visit to the field where Meriwether raises blooded horses, a look at the Negro quarters, and a long digression concerning the Southern defense of the slave system. The final narrative segment of the book is an account of Abe, a young Swallow Barn slave who goes bad but who redeems himself by losing his life while attempting to aid a vessel during a storm on the Chesapeake. *Swallow Barn* then concludes with the departure of Littleton for his New York home; a postscript, written after his return, relates the marriage of Bel and Ned Hazard and the continuing tranquil life of all his friends in the Old Dominion.

Sketched out in this manner, *Swallow Barn* would indeed

seem to be what Kennedy called it in his 1851 preface—a volume that is "utterly unartistic in plot and structure." Certainly to the modern taste it is too bulky, too digressive, too anchored to literary prototypes. It is, furthermore, neither a pure work of the fancy nor an entirely trustworthy factual account of its announced subject of life on a Virginia plantation. Nevertheless, in spite of all its easily tabulated defects, it remains in other important ways one of the most engrossing books produced by an American in the 1830's.

For, as I have suggested, the modern reader may find the most basic meanings of *Swallow Barn* in the very "flaw" from which Kennedy wished to divert attention: the fact that neither he nor his fictional mouthpiece, Mark Littleton, could maintain a consistent stance. His proposal to sketch life in western Virginia as an amused spectator from the outside world could not be entirely excised; traces of this plan remained in the early versions of his opening chapters, even when he had decided to shift the locale to the Tidewater district and send his traveler to Hoppergallop House on the Rappahannock.[19] But the final choice of Littleton as narrator shows Kennedy already veering away from this detached and satirical point of view. For Littleton (like Kennedy) is *both* outsider and insider; he is a Northerner but also kinsman to a large, closely knit Southern clan. His independence weakens and his critical eye wavers; he finds himself extolling the life of the region as well as occasionally unmasking its faults and foibles.

What finally emerges from *Swallow Barn*, then, is a double attitude about society which tells much about the dilemma of the American writer who—at the critics' urging—did choose the native scene for his subject matter. Like others among his contemporaries, Kennedy had two disparate aims: to augment the small stock of native regional legend and to undercut this nostalgic regionalism in the service of nationalism and progress. As a writer who responded emotionally to Irving, he inclined toward portraying an "ancient," aristocratic, amiable Virginia; as a businessman who ranked national above sectional interest, he was concerned with exposing the dangers of a pride in state and family which led to exclusiveness.

As a result of the pulls upon him, part of *Swallow Barn* is legend-making and uncritical. It is backward-looking and "historical"; it counts upon our memory of literary models to supply an atmosphere of age, status, and solidarity. It praises individual liberty, rejoices in "characters," assesses slavery as chiefly a local problem, and opposes central government whenever its power is bent upon wiping out all regional peculiarities. From the other angle of vision, the book accepts the reality of man's progress and argues the necessity of further change; it satirizes the provinciality and folly of this closed society, lets its members damn themselves through their tirades against outside interference and internal improvements, and scorns cherished States' rights. Kennedy's difficulty in synthesizing his views was not, to be sure, merely literary; it was the nation's problem, one for which resolution would be sought in thirty years' time in the radical conflict of a civil war. The dichotomy of *Swallow Barn* thus does not cleave it apart; it contributes instead to an understanding of the tension in the mind of a man who could be drawn both to the Southern past and the national future.

It is important to note how Kennedy develops both his legend of Virginia and the satirical view which subverts it. The book begins and ends with allusions to Captain John Smith's adventures in the early colony. In Littleton's "Introductory Epistle," which recounts his voyage up the James River, he tells his correspondent of passing the ruins of the earliest permanent English settlement:

> You would have laughed to see into what a state of lady-like rapture I had worked myself in my eagerness to get a peep at Jamestown, with all my effervescence of romance kindled up by the renown of the unmatchable Smith. The steward of the boat pointed it out when we had nearly passed it—and lo! there it was—the buttress of an old steeple, a barren fallow, some melancholy heifers, a blasted pine, and, on its top, a desolate hawk's nest. What a splendid field for the fancy! What a carte blanche for a painter! With how many things might this little spot be filled! (16-17)

Toward the close of the book Littleton returns to this "splendid field for the fancy."[20] Forced by bad weather to delay his planned departure from Swallow Barn, he takes to the library where he rejoices in his discovery of an early seventeenth-century folio recounting the history of "the Renowned Captayne John Smith, with his travel and adventures in the Foure Quarters of the Earthe. . . . Also, what befell in his Endeavours towards the Planting of the Colonie of Virginia; and, in especiall, his Marvellous Prouess and Incredible Escapes amongst the Barbarous Salvages. . . ." (495)[21] Littleton recalls the strength of his boyhood admiration for the doughty Captain Smith; now, "on the spot where Smith had achieved some of his most gallant wonders," he is moved to canonize him as the "true knight," the exemplar of the chivalric virtues which Virginians have sought to preserve. Littleton has to struggle with doubts about the total authenticity of the old chronicle, but at last he concludes that —even if partly legend—the story still is more valuable for Americans than any dry factual history:

> The character of Smith, like the extraordinary incidents of his life, strikes me as approaching nearer to the invention of a fiction than that of any other real personage of history. There is in it so much plain sense, mingled with such glory of manhood; so much homely wisdom and dauntless bravery combined—so much chivalrous adventure, set off with so much honesty; so much humility, and yet so much to boast of—if his nature were vainglorious:—these qualities are all so well balanced in his composition that they have an epic consistency, and seem more like an imagination, than a reality. (500)

This comment can be applied to parts of *Swallow Barn* as well. Clearly it is "nearer to the invention of a fiction" than to authentic history in its hero-worshiping vision of the pioneers of the Virginia colony. Quite early in the book Kennedy offers his own version of the "Cavalier myth":

> [Virginia's] early population . . . consisted of gentlemen of good name and condition, who brought within her confines a solid fund of respectability and wealth. This race of men grew vigorous in her genial atmosphere; her cloudless skies quickened and enlivened their tempers, and, in two centuries, gradually matured the sober and thinking Englishman into that spirited, imaginative being who now inhabits the lowlands of this state. (70)

The merits which Kennedy celebrates thus stem directly from the Elizabethan gentleman-adventurer and the seventeenth-century Cavalier. What these special characteristics are he soon makes plain: pride in a long family line; personal honor; love of individual liberty; belief in property as the basis for an enduring social system; chivalric behavior toward women; conservatism in religion and philosophy; participation in the public affairs of the state; dislike of outside interference, especially that of a central government; recognition of an aristocracy of worth, founded upon inherited property and sustained by enslaved Negroes who, if properly treated, were far better off than they could be in a state of barbarism.

With the exception of actual ownership of slaves, these are, of course, also attributes of the English landed gentry; and now the reasons behind Kennedy's attraction to those writers (both English and American) who had admiringly depicted such a class become clearer. For America, the raw young republic with true greatness still rather a matter of hope than of accomplishment, needed reassurance through such associations with a lofty past. In the face of sneers from abroad, it had to be instructed in history, in tradition—even in pure legend—if it was to achieve the self-awareness and self-confidence that could dare anything. Irving and James K. Paulding had, in their New York area, uncovered the richness of the Dutch colonial period. Cooper had shown the rise of a native aristocrat in Judge Temple of *The Pioneers;* he would soon examine the history of the landed Littlepage family; and, through such characters, he commemorated the American's triumph over savage Indian and rugged wilderness. Simms, too, would shortly begin to seek out useful, patriotic materials in the Carolinas and in the border regions. It was Kennedy, though, who first fully comprehended the power of the legend of aristocratic Virginia. Although he could not repress his mirth at the pretentiousness of some of these offspring of the Cavaliers, he tried sincerely to give the gentlemanly ideal its due.

His formal spokesman for Old Virginia is not the man most directly involved in the actions of the plot, Ned Hazard, but Frank Meriwether, whose beliefs and personal foibles are recorded at some length in Chapter II. Though Meriwether is inclined to the vice of indolence and is typically a foe of mercantilism and internal improvements, he is nonetheless saluted by Kennedy as "a very model of landed gentlemen." He is a magistrate, a hospitable host, a stay-at-home who has "never been in New England." He is a raiser of blooded horses (themselves an aristocracy!); a high-churchman who properly does not trouble himself about points of faith (as does the family's lower-class Presbyterian tutor); and a man who admires above all else the genius of Virginia: "indeed, it is a familiar thing with him to speak of the aristocracy of talent as only inferior to that of the landed interest." This sounds like a satirical crack, and to a degree it is; but the "landed interest" was not a comic matter for Kennedy. For all his follies, Meriwether is a conservator of property rights, a leader who makes possible an ordered society. His opinions—even if occasionally flatly wrong from Kennedy's own standpoint—filter down to help mold public opinion; and his influence always works for a stable commonwealth.

The pervasiveness of the ideals of this gentry among all classes is particularly dramatized in a chapter describing the local celebration of the Fourth of July. The occasion is marked by a general gathering at the river landing, once the site of a prosperous foreign trade in tobacco. There Littleton overhears a lively discussion between one Sandy Walker, a waterman, and a "greasy gentleman in a blue coat" over the question of States' rights. Sandy has asked if Congress cannot, simply by passing a law, "'come and take a road of theirn any where they have a mind to, through any man's land?'" Not according to the Constitution, answers the other; and, besides, there's the possibility of nullification by the state. But Sandy persists in his dark forebodings, and this exchange between the two follows:

> "Things are getting worse and worse," replied the other. "I can see how it's going! Here, the first thing General Jackson did when he came in, he wanted to have the President elected for six years; and, by and by, they will want him for ten! and now they want to cut up our orchards and meadows, whether or no; that's just the way Bonaparte went on. What's the use of states if they are all to be cut up with canals and railroads and tariffs? No, no, gentlemen! you may depend, Old Virginny's not going to let Congress carry on in her day!"

"How can they help it?" asked Sandy.

"We hav'nt *fout* and bled," rejoined the other, taking out of his pocket a large piece of tobacco, and cutting off a quid, as he spoke in a somewhat subdued tone, "we hav'nt *fout* and bled for our liberties to have our posterity and their land circumcised after this rate, to suit the figaries of Congress. So let them try it when they will!"

When Littleton and Ned Hazard return to Swallow Barn in the evening, they recount this colloquy of the yeomanry to Meriwether; and Littleton adds, "from what Frank let fall,—for he grew grave on the subject,—I have reason to think that he has some fearful misgivings of the ambitious designs of the general government. He is decidedly of the state rights party" (162-65).

What most deeply bothers Meriwether is what is unspoken but clearly implied in the argument at the Landing: if Congress can build railroads and canals through sovereign states, can it not also assume that it has the power to outlaw slavery? This problem of the South's "peculiar institution" could hardly be dodged by Kennedy, though he tries to calm sectional antagonisms by what he takes to be a reasonable summation of the slaveholders' case. Through much of the book the plantation Negroes are merely presented as a contented and well-cared-for working class whose labors support the gracious life of the white tenants of Swallow Barn. But, in a chapter toward the end of the book in which Littleton describes a visit to the slave quarters, the issue is finally confronted directly. Littleton speaks in it as a Northerner whose prejudices have been shaken by direct observation; he has been surprised to discover that the slaves are not harshly treated, and indeed he is "quite sure they never could become a happier people than I find them here." They are in a transition state between barbarism and civilization, he muses; and, even in a condition of bondage, they have greater safety and individual dignity than do many seamen or soldiers. Repeating some of these notions to Meriwether, Littleton draws from him an unexpectedly conciliatory discourse:

"The world," said he, "has begun very seriously to discuss the evils of slavery, and the debate has sometimes, unfortunately, been levelled to the comprehension of our negroes, and pains have been taken that it should reach them. [Meriwether is, of

> course, referring to abolition societies.] . . . Ingenious men, some of them not very honest, have found . . . themes for agitation and popular appeal in all ages. How likely are they to find, in this question of slavery, a theme for the highest excitement; and, especially, how easy it is to inflame the passions of these untutored and unreckoning people, our black population, with the subject! For slavery, as an original question, is wholly without justification or defence. It is theoretically and morally wrong—and fanatical and one-sided thinkers will call its continuance, even for a day, a wrong, under any modification of it. But, surely, if these people are consigned to our care by the accident, or, what is worse, the premeditated policy which has put them upon our commonwealth, the great duty that is left to us is, to shape our conduct in reference to them, by a wise and beneficent consideration of the case as it exists, and to administer wholesome laws for their government, making their servitude as tolerable to them as we can consistently with our own safety and their ultimate good. We should not be justified in taking the hazard of internal convulsions to get rid of them; nor have we a right, in the desire to free ourselves, to whelm them in greater evils than their present bondage. A violent removal of them, or a general emancipation, would assuredly produce one or the other of these calamities. . . ." (455-56)

Meriwether proceeds to argue that any program of emancipation should be exclusively from the South, and he assures Littleton that slaveholders neither like the present system nor find it profitable. He even has some suggestions for immediate improvement of the slave code. Families, he concedes, should never be split apart (a crime which Mrs. Stowe would later charge against the South in *Uncle Tom's Cabin*); moreover, he would select a few of the older and more trustworthy men and form them into a "feudatory"—in effect, serfs who could work for themselves as tenant farmers. This talk between Meriwether and Littleton is followed by their visit to the cabin of "old mammy Lucy," and we are given the interpolated history of her son Abe, in which the rectitude of honorable masters is exhibited through a cloyingly sentimental tale.

Inevitably, though, a personal uneasiness undercuts these passages of sweet reasonableness. While actually writing *Swallow Barn,* Kennedy was himself briefly a master; and he was driven to make a compromise decision. Sending off his servant Sam (who had proved untrustworthy) to be sold in Virginia, he vowed in his journal: "I will never own another slave, and should not have taken this fellow if he had not been given to me by my father."[22] He could not in conscience affirm that one man could hold lawful title to another; the real problem, however, was not the legality of slavery but the disposal of it without totally disrupting Southern society. Still echoing Meriwether, Kennedy struggled with the question, as a passage in a much later journal reveals:

> Manifestly *emancipation* would be a greater evil than the continuance of slavery. I mean, *rapid emancipation*. We should ruin the slave, and make desolate the slave country. Our duty therefore is to mitigate the evil by cautious and discreet treatment of it, and to aid the progress of natural causes in the gradual obliteration of slavery, which is inevitable in the course of the growth of the country. . . .[23]

And here, in brief, was the whole puzzling conflict which had run through *Swallow Barn:* the status quo versus change, the nostalgia for an achieved order versus the inevitability of its dissolution. Kennedy had done his best for the world of old Virginia, but he ultimately refused to accept that past as a true Golden Age. The legend of Captain John Smith, the Cavalier, and the old aristocracy was an appealing one; and Americans of his own day ought to be taught to take pride in it. But the Old Dominion was doomed; it would pass because many of its ideals already had shrunk into empty formalism. To see this fact was to return to the satirical viewpoint with which he had begun; he could not, finally, erase it from his book.

Kennedy's specific criticism is founded upon that very characteristic of Virginia which contributed to its virtues—the fact that it had stayed a closed and self-sufficient society. If family ties and the holding of inherited property gave stability to the social order, that order was achieved at the risk of excessive conservatism, of drifting out of the mainstream of national life into Lotus Land. Pride in ancestry easily became snobbishness; the chivalric code could fade into the weak sentimentalism which admired only the far-off and the long-ago; the iron grip on every acre of the patrimonial lands could become a mere fetish. Kennedy's sharpest barbs are directed toward the exclusiveness of community at the expense of acceptance of the greater America. Though he was emotionally stirred by the defender of individual liberty and regional rights, he could not concede the power of a state to defy acts designed for the general good. The pastoral condition of Virginia, pleasantly innocent as it seemed to the visitor, ought *not* to be preserved forever, since it conduced to ignorance and isolation.

Kennedy's sketch of a small hamlet near Swallow Barn shows his disgust at the shiftlessness of such backward areas. Having described the main establishments—a wheelwright's shop and a country general store—he adds this ironic observation: "As may readily be conjectured, this mart of custom was not without its due proportion of that industrious, thriving, and reputable class of comers who laudably devote their energies to disputation, loud swearing, bets and whisky,—a class which, to the glory of our land, is surprisingly rife in every country side" (359-60). In this village Ned Hazard encounters and bests a swaggerer who accosts him; and this drunken bully is made an object lesson for those who hold that the status of a gentleman is sufficient in itself and does not demand concomitant duties:

> This man had been originally educated in liberal studies, and had commenced his career not without some character in the country, but had fallen into disgrace through vicious habits. An unfortunate reputation for brilliant talents, in early life, had misled him into the belief that the care by which a good name is won and preserved is a useless virtue, and that self-control is a tax which only men of inferior parts pay for success. This delusion brought about the usual penalties; first, disappointment, then debauch, and after that, in a natural sequence, the total wreck of worldly hopes. . . . (361)

Indeed, all the gentlemen of *Swallow Barn* are in some way infected by the system to which they give service. Meriwether's talents and charm shine brightly enough at home, but they are untested outside of the state; his model of behavior is that of the

English landed gentleman as memorialized in fiction, and it is plain that it is a self-centered ideal which is oblivious of the growing republic. Old Mr. Tracy is completely bound by a ruling passion—his right to inherited property—and the lawsuit plot line exposes how ridiculous this possessiveness can become. The claim which he wants settled is to a useless bit of swamp, and he knows it. All that matters is that ground which originally belonged to The Brakes be again established as his by legal recognition. Swansdown has degenerated into a fop—one who comprehends only false culture and obsolescent rituals of behavior.

Virginian admiration for the Roman soldierly ideal is ridiculed through Philly Wart, who had commanded a troop during the War of 1812 called the "Invincible Blues." Wart speaks with great pride of his patriotic service during a dinner party scene; but under Ned Hazard's needling he is driven to concede that, though his troop had many alarms, it never actually managed to engage the enemy. " 'Well,' " comments Harvey Riggs, who is a cousin of Bel Tracy, " 'it was a very gallant thing, take it altogether. . . . So, gentleman, fill your glasses. Here's to Captain Wart of the Invincible Blues, the genuine representative of the chivalry of the Old Dominion!' " (344)

But Kennedy's sharpest satire of the decay of the chivalric ideal is reserved for the ladies of Swallow Barn and The Brakes. Bel Tracy's proclaimed expectation of life is derived from what she had read in romances; we see how far she has gone when she tries to train a hawk according to the rules of medieval falconers. She also endeavors to persuade poor-white Hafen Blok to act as her minstrel, even contriving a proper costume for him. But Hafen's rough and bloody traditional ballads are not to the taste of a girl who has fed on the minstrelsy of Sir Walter Scott. Attempting once to please her, he suggests—to her dismay—that he render

> " 'the Gosport Tragedy,' that shows how a young damsel was led astray by a ship's carpenter, and carried into a lonesome wood; and how her ghost haunted him at sea;—
> " 'When he *immediantly* fell on his knees,
> And the blood in his veins with horror did freeze.' " (379)

Kennedy delights in this kind of verbal fooling, and his ear is sharp for inanely pretentious dialogue. One of his best satiric scenes occurs in Chapter XXX, in which Prudence Meriwether and Catharine Tracy moon over the elegant Swansdown; neither at first suspects that he has made advances to each of them. Prudence rhapsodizes over Swansdown's role in the land suit:

> "He had the art," she said, "to impart a charm to the dullest subjects. His discrimination was intuitive, and facilitated his journey through the mazes of research, like one that wandered over a shorn meadow. Who but a man of genius could unravel the occult darkness of the boundary line, and shed certainty, in one day, upon an important question, in opposition to all the courts and all the lawyers of a state that boasted of both, with that forensic jurist Mr. Wart (manifestly prejudiced against his opinion) on the other side. There was a moral romanticity in it. It was like casting a spell of 'gramarie' over his opponents. The world would talk of this thing hereafter!"
>
> "It is very surprising," muttered Catharine.
>
> "Think of it, my dear!" cried Prudence. "The country, before long, will discover his dormant talents, and he will be compelled to forego his reluctance to guide the destinies of his native state."
>
> "It can be nothing but his modesty," rejoined Kate, "that keeps him in the background now. He never would have been beaten three times for Congress, if he had not been so diffident." (298-99)

Few other writers besides Kennedy in the America of this period could so neatly have hit off in such a brief passage so many foibles: intellectual pretension, meaningless legal wrangles, romantic yearnings, rhetorical flourish—in short, the self-revelations of a society which preferred façade to backbone, lofty words and manners to workaday deeds, literary posturing to solid character. And yet for twenty years he remained split between his amused reaction to a provincial society that fancied itself so grand and his appreciation of the legend of the grandeur of Virginia's past.

In his 1832 preface Kennedy bade his readers to choose their own emphasis; he sheltered himself, he said, behind the motto on the title page, taken from the prologue to the *Morte D'Arthur:* "And, for to pass the time, this book shall be pleasant to read in. But for to give faith and believe all is true that is contained therein, ye be at your own liberty." Yet, when he revised *Swallow Barn* in the early 1850's, he found he wished to soften the satirical tone to some degree; he now expressed regret that "progress" had brought innovation so quickly to Virginia. "The whole surface of society," according to his new preface, was "exhibiting the traces of a process by which it is likely to be rubbed down, in time, to one level, and varnished with the same gloss." What had once been authentically and individualistically American seemed to him "already to be dissolving into a mixture which affects us unpleasantly as a tame and cosmopolitan substitute for the old warmth and salient vivacity of our ancestors." And so he could now, with a different stress, reassert the fidelity of his sketches and hope for their preservation as records: "They have already begun to assume the tints of a relic of the past, and may, in another generation, become archaeological, and sink into the chapter of antiquities."

It is hardly likely that the professional historian of the twentieth century would see them in quite this light. But *Swallow Barn* remains a true document in another sense: it is a valid reflection of the divided mind of John Pendleton Kennedy, a man who looked forward but understood the pragmatic value of legend—one who, like many of his countrymen, yearned for roots in the past and for the America that was to be, and was not at all sure how the two could be reconciled.

CHAPTER 3

Horse-Shoe Robinson: The Price of Progress

I *In Demand*

AS SOON AS HENRY C. CAREY, Kennedy's publisher, was convinced that *Swallow Barn* would show a profit, he began entreating his new author to capitalize on his first success. Throughout the spring of 1832 Carey regularly hinted that a second book "by the author of *Swallow Barn*" would increase the sales of the volume; some months later he was blatantly appealing to Kennedy's vanity: "Irving will write little—Cooper says he will write no more—& I fear we shall shortly see our lights extinguished, unless you take & keep the field."[1] But Kennedy, though he clearly yearned to keep the readership he had captured, found that his other duties constantly interrupted the hours he had hoped to set aside for writing; and *Horse-Shoe Robinson,* which would be his first regular novel, did not appear until 1835.

Kennedy's journals and letterbooks record his slow progress. On October 11, 1832, he noted simply, "Began Horse Shoe Robinson this evening."[2] A month later he commented that he had given the past fortnight to the book but was still unsure of his ultimate direction: "I don't know how the story will turn out—for I am writing it at present in the most hurried and imperfect form in order that when its framework is all together I may judge of its effect, and finish it to my liking. I have finished about a fourth of the first volume." By December he was referring to the growing manuscript as "Mildred Lindsay" (the story's heroine) and was jotting down progress reports, but his journal also laments his inability to keep steadily at it.

Kennedy was not, of course, a professional writer who had to rely, as did Simms, upon regular publication; he still had his law practice, and he was often in Washington in these months representing business interests in the agitation over new tariff legislation. He was also reveling in being the literary lion and the prominent man-about-town, one who was called upon to lend a hand in various civic functions. One of these extra duties would profoundly affect the literary career of a more gifted man, Edgar Allan Poe. In the summer of 1833 Kennedy was one of the judges in a contest sponsored by a local periodical, the *Saturday Visiter*. Poe, then living in poverty in Baltimore with his aunt, submitted a poem and several stories; the $50 prize was awarded for his "MS. Found in a Bottle." Kennedy shortly thereafter befriended Poe and was influential in getting him the post of editor of the distinguished Richmond magazine, the *Southern Literary Messenger;* Poe, not always grateful to his benefactors, never forgot the kindness of the man whose reputation originally far outshone his own.[3]

But, despite the calls of business and of his other affairs, Kennedy somehow managed to find time to add to the increasing pile of draft copy. On December 15, 1833, he jotted down the fact that he had begun the second volume of the new story, having finished the first one five days earlier. Carey was delighted to hear of such progress and offered to publish the tale on a fifty-fifty profit-sharing basis—though he prudently cautioned Kennedy not to expect substantial royalties until his name became better known. Kennedy, however, continued to proceed slowly through what eventually was to be an extremely long manuscript; and nearly a year passed before he entered in his journal for October 30, 1834, the statement that he had "nearly finished" his book. He then wrote to Carey, offering his own terms for publication: he would have the type set in Baltimore so that he could inspect proofs more conveniently; he wanted $1,000 for an edition of two thousand copies and an extra one-quarter of that sum if the second thousand copies sold out. By the first of January, 1835, the writing was at last completed; on that date he recorded that he had "put it to press." By this time, too, Carey had promised him $1,200 for an edition of three thousand copies; and the English publisher Richard Bentley had contracted to issue it abroad on a mutually agreeable basis.

Overruling Carey's intention to release the new work in the autumn, when he felt there would be a better market, Kennedy pressed ahead with his correction of the proofs; and on June 20 the book was published simultaneously by Carey in Philadelphia and Bentley in London in order to forestall the pirates who had snapped up *Swallow Barn.* The American edition Kennedy dedicated to Irving; the British one, to the well-known poet Samuel Rogers. Sales in America were gratifying; but Carey, appalled by the length of the book (which cut into profits), demanded some pruning before issuing second and third printings. In England, however, Bentley gloomily reported that the "anti-Anglican feeling pervading the work" had destroyed its market potential and left him with a loss of about £150. But, despite this setback abroad, *Horse-Shoe Robinson* rapidly boosted Kennedy's reputation; by the end of 1835 he could exult both in favorable reviews and in many private letters of congratulation from already prominent American writers.

II *The National Epic*

It had taken Kennedy far longer than he had supposed necessary to see his words again in print. But a study of the many notes which he made during the composition of *Horse-Shoe* suggests that it was not outside commitments alone which delayed its completion. As had been the case with *Swallow Barn,* his materials proved to be more complex than he had anticipated; thematic conflicts emerged which could not be ignored or simply written around. What was conceived as a thrilling tale of the national epic period—the War of Independence—became, in part at least, an inquiry into the meaning of American history itself.

Almost inevitably, Kennedy had determined at the outset to cast his second book in the form of a historical romance, the subgenre which was now the rage in nationalist-minded America. The Revolution had, of course, long been recognized as the preeminent national story. But, as Kennedy pointed out in his original preface to *Horse-Shoe,* so long as knowledge of the war had remained in living memories, it had seemed too recent and even too obvious a subject for celebration in fiction. After the fiftieth anniversary in 1826, however, that objection had "been nullified by common consent,—that being deemed the fair poetical limit which converts tradition into truth, and takes away all right of contradiction from a surviving actor in the scene."[4]

And so American writers, eager to make native fiction predominantly patriotic, had recently been refighting the war with the fervor of their forebears. Cooper had originally planned a series of thirteen romances about the Revolution, each to be set in one of the original colonies; John Neal, Lydia Maria Child, and others had regaled their audiences with suitably heroic tales. But, except in a peripheral way, none of these authors had touched the subject of the British campaign to subjugate the Southern colonies, or had they chronicled the events which led to the surrender of Cornwallis at Yorktown. This topic was Kennedy's discovery, and part of the success of his book was no doubt owing to the originality of its setting; though—as Kennedy could not have known at the time—Simms was at this very moment independently embarking upon his own regional interpretation of the Revolutionary struggle.

Kennedy's attraction to events in the South during this period appears to have been entirely fortuitous and not the result of any prolonged search for new materials for his fiction. A number of his Virginian Pendleton ancestors had distinguished themselves during Revolutionary days; he had already drawn from family tradition and the personal memory of war veterans for several characters in *Swallow Barn:* the patriotic Hazards, the Tory Tracys, the common soldiers like Hafen Blok and Mike Brown. In *Horse-Shoe Robinson* Kennedy set down as the actual germ of the story an incident which had occurred some years earlier during his visit to South Carolina.[5] According to the more embellished version, which he presented in his preface to the 1852 revised edition, he had in 1819 been investigating a land claim in an isolated section when he met by chance the aged veteran who would give his name to the book. Pressed to recount his wartime activities, Horse Shoe had delighted him with a racy narration which occupied a full evening—and then Kennedy had seen him no more. But, so the preface continues, "I made a record of what he told me, whilst the memory of it was still fresh, and often afterwards reverted to it, when accident or intentional research brought into my view events connected with the times and scenes to which his story had reference" (10). Finally, Kennedy informs the reader, after his book was first published, he had received a comforting testimonial from a friend who at his request had taken a copy to Robinson, then living in Alabama. "It is all true and right," Horse Shoe is supposed to have said—"excepting about them women, which I disremember."

Nevertheless, Kennedy's account can be accepted only with marked reservations. He did indeed see a man whose name he put down as Horse Shoe Robinson during his trip to South Carolina, and he probably listened to some anecdotes: the episode is recorded in a chronology that is carried only through the year 1822, and the Kennedy papers contain other references to this meeting. But the connection between this man—whose actual name appears to have been James Robertson—and the character of the book is only minimal; neither their ages nor their wartime experiences match, and the nickname Horse Shoe was not acquired by Robertson until *after* the war. Attempts to link other major characters of the book to historical figures similarly fail to convince; even a cursory glance at the manuscript materials reveals that Kennedy changed the names of his principals several times and that the plot of the story as published differs significantly from the original concept. In spite of Kennedy's own conventional protestations to the contrary, the book must be approached as a fiction, as only partially bound by fact; it cannot be relied upon as authentic history.[6]

It is, of course, true that Kennedy set *Horse-Shoe Robinson* against the backdrop of a real epoch: the year 1780, which saw the fall of Charleston to the British and the general domination of the Southern colonies by enemy troops and their local sympathizers. This period of the "Tory ascendancy" (as the book is subtitled) provided many events and situations which could be transmuted into the staples of a historical romance: families had been sundered by opposing political loyalties; partisan bands were making daring raids on the British regulars; and the spirit of liberty was being kept alive in the face of great odds by leaders like Sumter, Marion, and Pickens. But such materials had to be unified by means of a running narrative, and Kennedy's manuscript notes disclose his struggle in inventing a regular fictional plot after the models of Scott and Cooper. Inevitably there would have to be a central love story; what he quickly saw was that he could inject the familiar motif of love versus duty by making his couple a dashing American officer and the daughter of a gentleman whose sympathies had remained with the British. The main incidents of the plot, then, could turn upon the captivities and escapes of the hero as he strove to further the Revolutionary cause in the very camps of the enemy.

At various times before he began actual composition, Kennedy set down plot summaries, or scenarios, which blocked out the overall action. One early version posits these steps (the names supplied in brackets are those which Kennedy gave to these characters in the published version):

1. The courtship and secret of marriage of Carril [Arthur Butler] & Caroline [Mildred Lindsay].
2. A lapse of four years. Carril and Horse Shoe Robinson travelling in the mountains—their stop at Wat Adair, the Prophecy.
3. Carril's capture and Horse Shoe's escape.
4. Burnside [?]—the education of Henry [Henry Lindsay]—Fothergill [Philip Lindsay, father of Henry and Mildred] &c.
5. Caroline and Henry riding—they are met by Horse Shoe.
6. Caroline's journey [presumably to aid her captured lover].
7. Carril's escape.
8. Difficulties.
9. The gathering of the forces ag[ainst] Ferguson [a British officer].
10. Fothergill's pursuit of his daughter; his joining Ferguson—
11. The Battle of King's Mountain. Death of Fothergill.[7]

As Kennedy continued to ponder his story line, he realized that he could strengthen narrative interest by casting some mystery over the true relationship of the hero and heroine:

"I think it would be better to present Caroline and Carril throughout in the character of lovers without making any allusion to their secret marriage, and then to clear up the mystery of her behavior [in her daring attempts to free him], by giving at the end of the tale their correspondence in 1779 in which the private marriage is disclosed." To create an air of verisimilitude he resolved that the story should be told by the pseudonymous Mark Littleton of *Swallow Barn,* as if he had drawn it directly "from personal narrative, and the letters of the parties."

Other notes develop an idea which was later discarded: "Carril should be killed in the action at King's Mountain and the tale should possess a tragic interest—revealing a history of an unconsummated marriage. The prophecy [mentioned in point 2, above] should allude to this. . . ." Then comes his decision to change the names, a fact sufficient to prove that he had no historical prototypes in mind: "Instead of Fothergill & Carril, I shall call them Lindsay and Butler—My heroine shall be Mildred Lindsay." And finally there is his second thought about the fate of his hero: "I don't think I can afford to kill Butler. . . ." He certainly could not in a popular romance; readers of the day would have been outraged at having their expectations thus radically defeated. And so Kennedy transferred a noble death in action from his hero to a subordinate character (John Ramsay) and created the pathetic figure of Mary Musgrove to be the bereaved sweetheart. Further, he dropped the "prophecy" element, though some baffling traces of it remain in the published version. With these alterations of original plan, the main plot was now fixed; and little more was added or changed during the period of actual writing.

Kennedy's working notes are fascinating for their evidence as to how much he remained under the domination of his literary models—indeed, how unlikely it was in the 1830's that any American writer would attempt startling innovations either in plot or method of narration. The basic structure of the historical romance had already become as stylized as the popular Western is today. It would, for example, place fictional characters on the fringe of a stirring action in the nation's annals; it would focus on an upper-class hero and heroine whose foreordained union would be delayed by parental interference, forced separation, or any other obstacle which the novelist could think up; it would provide for the hero a lower-class retainer who would ride with him on his adventures and help to engineer his escapes from frequent captivities; it would supply enough local color to satisfy the demand for a recognizably American terrain; it would grant its female readers frequent opportunities for the romantic flush, the fluttered heart, the sentimental tear.

For these and other expected devices Kennedy needed no more than an acquaintance with Scott, Cooper, and the host of blatant imitators who found the formulas easy to adopt and profitable to manipulate. For historical and factual detail, Kennedy required only a standard history and reference to some of the many volumes of reminiscences and anecdotes concerning the Revolution which had appeared by this date.[8] He could, furthermore, draw upon personal knowledge of parts of Virginia and South Carolina for his settings, and he could summon up his own youthful experiences in the War of 1812 for scenes of army life. *Swallow Barn* had also been useful apprentice work for the new book, for in the earlier work he had already sketched out the Tory, the patriotic Southern landowner, the hot-blooded hero, the spirited heroine, and those prototypes of Horse Shoe—Hafen Blok and Mike Brown. Yet Kennedy in the end lacked the utilitarian narrative skill of a Cooper or a Simms; he could not match either in the multiplication of exciting incidents; and *Horse-Shoe Robinson,* on the basis of story line alone, strikes the modern reader as slow-moving and needlessly prolix.

Purely in terms of plot, the chief structural flaw of the book is that its nominal hero, Major Arthur Butler, languishes in captivity during the action of thirty-eight out of the fifty-eight chapters. He is rescued only once and is quickly recaptured; and he even manages to be still in enemy hands during the climactic event, the Battle of King's Mountain. The function of keeping the story moving therefore devolves upon Horse Shoe and Henry and Mildred Lindsay, who spend their time striving either to free Butler or to keep him from being shot as a traitor by his British captors. Furthermore, Kennedy's two carefully preserved "secrets" evoke no sustained interest and provide no startling surprises. The first—that Butler and Mildred have been man and wife for some time before the action of th opens—is a mild fillip at best. The second involves the mysterious character called Tyrrel, a Tory who is the archenemy of Butler and the would-be lover of Mildred. Tyrrel is revealed to be the British Captain St. Jermyn, who has pretended to befriend Butler during the latter's long bondage but has actually been working to get him condemned for a supposed plot against Philip Lindsay. A more experienced writer of popular romance would have had St. Jermyn brought to his deserved ignominious end by the sword of Butler himself, but Kennedy rather inexplicably lets his villain meet his death by hanging after the concluding battle. St. Jermyn is executed by revenge-hungry Whigs, and only by chance does Butler come across his body. Recognizing him as his erstwhile friendly captor and being informed at this moment that he was the person who masqueraded under the name of Tyrrel, Butler can only exclaim: "Tyrrel and St. Jermyn the same person! This is a strange mystery". (549) It is, indeed, since it is a rather pointless one; St. Jermyn's chance, off-stage death immediately renders him of no further concern to Butler or anyone else. The "mystery" has turned out to be mystification for its own sake.

But it must at once be reiterated that, while the plot of *Horse-Shoe Robinson* as mere plot may only bore the modern reader, the thematic conflicts embedded in its story do much to redeem Kennedy's ineptness. For, finally, this book is seriously concerned with divided allegiances—with choices which must be made between the past and the future, between the old homeland and the rising nation, between the father and the husband. It mirrors a world of internal conflict, of native-born Americans who are combatting one another as well as an enemy from outside. It therefore extends further back in time some of the fundamental issues raised in *Swallow Barn;* once again it exposes the quandary of a writer who sought to make a coherent pattern out of the past of his nation. Kennedy is implicitly asking: What had the revolutionists set as their goal in a new society? Had something of value to die in order that the country might be born anew? For all his strong desire to match his contemporaries in the glorification of our epic age, his Iliad passes beyond celebration into a conceptual dilemma.

III *The Cost of Change*

Kennedy's sense of dissident ideals is made explicit in the opening pages of *Horse-Shoe Robinson,* in which he offers a "topographical discourse" on his setting—the South Garden region of the Virginia mountains. Partly, this section is the leisurely scene-painting conventional in historical romance; partly, too, it represents his effort to extol the native landscape as proper material for fiction. But, as in *Swallow Barn,* his focus shifts as he scans the "narrow passes," "romantic dells," and "fearful crags"; beneath the physical aspects of the land lie layers of earlier history and legend—a past now largely buried by the upheavals which marked the Revolutionary era. As late as 1780 (the date of his story), Kennedy muses, this land was still the domain of aristocrats:

> A rich soil, a pure atmosphere, and great abundance of wood and water, to say nothing of the sylvan beauties of the mountain, possessed a great attraction for the wealthy proprietors of the low country; and the land was, therefore, generally parcelled out in large estates held by opulent owners, whose husbandry did not fail, at least, to accumulate in profusion the comforts of life, and afford full scope to that prodigal hospitality, which, at that period even more than at present, was the boast of the state. The laws of primogeniture exercised their due influence on the national habits; and the odious division of property amongst undeserving younger brothers, whom our modern philosophy would fain persuade us have as much merit, and as little capacity to thrive in the world as their elders, had not yet formed part of the household thoughts of these many-acred squires. . . .
>
> Since that period, well-a-day! the hand of the reaper has put in his sickle upon divided fields; crowded progenies have grown up under these paternal roof-trees; daughters have married and brought in strange names; the subsistence of one has been spread into the garner of ten; the villages have grown populous; the University [of Virginia] has lifted up its didactic head; and everywhere over this abode of ancient wealth, the hum of industry is heard in the carol of the ploughman, the echo of the wagoner's whip, the rude song of the boatman, and in the clatter of the mill. Such are the mischievous interpolations of the republican system! (15)

The central thematic conflict of Kennedy's story is clearly announced in this passage. Nationhood quite properly brought to America a progressive spirit, a free and open society, and the benefits of industry. But there had been a loss too: of roots in an older culture, of "prodigal hospitality," of a structured social order, of property tied by law to family lines. Change, then, means a gain—but at the expense of some cherished aspect of life which cannot be salvaged. As Mildred Lindsay discovers, to win a husband is to lose a father; to leave home is to give allegiance to another house. Thus Kennedy manages to convey still what it was like for an American—in the 1830's as well as in the 1780's—to be aware of his dual inheritance: European and colonial, landed gentry and yeoman, isolated farm and commercial city; in short, nostalgia for the past or acceptance of a revolution which brought a changed order.

As in *Swallow Barn,* Kennedy develops these themes slowly, relying in the opening section more on extended character analyses than on action to draw the reader into the story. The first eleven chapters, set in the Virginia Blue Ridge, are largely a prologue to the main narrative; their function is to introduce the three members of the Lindsay family, as well as Major Butler and his traveling companion, Horse Shoe. Philip Lindsay, a wealthy gentleman, has tried to escape involvement in the war, while remaining steadfastly loyal to the crown; his daughter Mildred, however, has given her heart to Butler; and Lindsay's young son Henry is equally a rebel against the past. Kennedy devotes many pages to a dissection of Philip Lindsay since the division within his home is an epitome of the main lines of argument in the book.

Clearly Philip Lindsay is the incarnation of the Tory attitude toward America; an early manuscript note concerning him flatly states: "Lindsay's character [is] to exhibit the principles of a man attached to aristocratic rule, and absolutism. A scorn for popular judgment, a disposition to predict the ultimate downfall of a government which rests power in the people."[9] Yet, while he is manifestly wrong in his beliefs, he is far from villainous in his conduct; indeed, as Kennedy finally portrayed him, he is a weak rather than an evil man. Born in Virginia to a good family and educated in England, Lindsay had returned to

America to marry an heiress and settle into the easy life which wealth and position afforded the country gentleman. But the outbreak of the war and the sudden death of his wife had driven him to take up residence in his summer mountain retreat, a "neat and comfortable rustic dwelling" which he calls the Dove Cote. There, in an effort to temper his personal sorrows, he now devotes himself to his long-time enthusiasm for the "obsolete subtleties of the old schools of philosophy"; his well-stocked library, Kennedy notes disapprovingly, "furnished a curious index to this unhealthy appetite for the marvellous and the mystical" (82), which has led him to fear some power has his daughter in thrall.[10] Lindsay's self-exile has been attained at great personal cost; since he was a known loyalist, his estates were subject to confiscation, and he has had to transfer the Dove Cote to Mildred and invest the proceeds from his other property in England. His remaining hope is that he can escape in his isolated home the unpleasantness of a war which he fears will see the eventual triumph of the revolutionists.

Kennedy betrays his own sympathy for the life of retirement, ease, and refinement which he imagines a man like Lindsay might have led; and he allows himself a rather surprising comment which can be explained only by the conflicts within his own nature and his desire to glorify a distant past in which his countrymen might still take some pride. The neighborhood surrounding the Dove Cote, he remarks, "furnished an intelligent and hospitable society; and the great western wilderness smiled with the contentment of a refined and polished civilization, which no after day in the history of this empire has yet surpassed—perhaps, not equaled" (84). But to live thus is, for Kennedy, to disregard the necessary duty of an upper class: to serve actively the social order in which one believes. Lindsay, therefore, is not allowed to shun his own obligations; he cannot turn away the Tories who are working upon him in the effort to divert his wealth and his personal ability to their plots against the rebel leaders. Lindsay is thus torn: not only because he genuinely prefers quiet and noninvolvement but also because he learns from their lips that his children, the new generation of the old province, have become strong partisans of the drive for independence.

As the plot develops, however, Lindsay is finally persuaded by the underhanded Tory who calls himself Tyrrel to go with him to South Carolina to join other wealthy adherents of the crown; Tyrrel not unnaturally also has his eye on Mildred and her own expectations of wealth. Because recent British victories have given Lindsay unforeseen hope, he makes the trip, thereby leaving the way open for Mildred and Henry to go in search of the captive Butler. But Lindsay's long-delayed activism has come too late to save either his cause or himself. Tyrrel's scheme to bring together the civilian loyalists fails, and Lindsay's last concern in life is to find the daughter he now knows (by means of a letter from her) to be the wife of a rebel leader. Pursuing her, he is caught in the culminating Battle of King's Mountain; and, ironically, the man who tried to evade the horrors of war receives a mortal wound from a stray bullet. Only when close to the moment of death is he reconciled; with Butler and his children around him, he at last acknowledges the inevitability of change: "'I have foreseen this day, and felt its coming; . . . it has happened as it was ordained. I have unwisely struggled against my doom'" (545). The loyalist thus meets a deservedly violent end. But it is not loyalty to Britain in itself that is condemned here; Kennedy cannot portray all Britons or Tories as base in their motivations since he recognizes the importance to Americans of their ancient ties to England. Lindsay simply did not assume his obligation to fight for a cause he felt to be right: as a gentleman, he was a "man to hate what is base," but he was also one who fatally chose "to stand apart from the mass, as one who will not have his virtue tainted" (96).

And so Lindsay dies in order that his daughter and son may be free to play their foreordained roles in a new nation. Only this thematic concern gives to Mildred and Henry any life or kindles any interest in them as characters; like their father, they are abstractions and not figures in the round. In external appearance and manner, Mildred especially is another of the wax dolls of historical romance. Her only unconventional behavior is her unmaidenly daring in riding into occupied territory to save Butler, and Kennedy removes even this minor titillation by solemnly assuring us that her indecorousness is to be excused in a *wife* (388). Henry—perhaps because he is too young to be burdened with a love affair—scores somewhat higher in the scale of verisimilitude. But, like his sister, he is functional rather than individual; he links the best of the past order—his father's bearing, intelligence, and grace—to the best which the new America can offer: a place in which he can be his own man and not just his father's son.

Kennedy's absorption in the problems raised by the split within Lindsay's family carries over into his portrayal of the formal hero of the novel, Major Butler. Like a hundred archetypes, he is endowed with good looks, manly physique, good family, and noble bearing. But Kennedy significantly alters the formula; Butler is also introduced as "a native of one of the lower districts of South Carolina, [who is] already the possessor, by inheritance, of what was then called a handsome fortune" (87). As Southern Gentleman from another "ancient" American region, then, he is the proper foil for that older aristocrat, Philip Lindsay. Butler's homeland too is overrun by an enemy and his estates have been confiscated, but he will not choose the easy way of sequestered noninvolvement. Every hope which he has for his country's future depends upon the recovery of his property and the restoration of his own sort of ruling class after the enemy has been expelled; to fight is a duty which he could not dream of shirking. As the book opens, Butler is under orders to proceed to his native state to encourage the partisan efforts in destroying the British strongholds dominating the South. But he is captured rather early in the main actions of the tale and does not regain his freedom (except for one short-lived bolt) until the next-to-last chapter. Kennedy would thus appear to defeat his own purpose in building up the character of the patriotic Butler, since his hero rarely can act at his own will and must expend most of his ingenuity in trying to keep himself from being summarily executed.

But Butler's plight is to be understood as representing both the military frustration of the patriots during the "Tory ascendancy" and the still enslaving power of the colonial era. He cannot be permitted to die, as Kennedy had initially schemed, because his most valuable role is *yet* to come: he must be a leader in the nation which will be created at the war's end. His liberation, then, at the moment of the decisive Battle of King's Mountain signifies, first, the freeing of his homeland; joined with the death of Lindsay, it also suggests the release of the past's hold on Butler himself. For he has been intimately involved with the old-school Lindsay family, having met, wooed, and won Mildred at the very beginning of the revolution. Under other circumstances he might well have been welcomed into her circle and settled down among the Virginia landed gentry. But the war has exposed their antithetical philosophies and forced Butler into an ambivalent attitude toward Mildred's parents. Like Lindsay, he thinks of himself as a born aristocrat and a natural leader; and he equally supports property as the basis of social order. But, unlike his father-in-law, who shrinks from contacts with the common herd and loses himself instead in mind-sapping speculations, Butler draws strength and knowledge from his lower-class aide, Horse Shoe Robinson; and he scorns affectation in his treatment of any rank. Thematically considered, Butler is the Southern Gentleman in bondage, literally wedded to an aristocratic past and aware of his own privileged station, but also looking toward his freedom in the new society which can be achieved only with the co-operation of men like his faithful scout.

Kennedy thus tempers his longing for an aristocracy of wealth with his attraction to that ever-resourceful "natural" man for whom, after all, the book is named. Although Kennedy claimed that he had based his fictional character directly upon the real-life Revolutionary veteran whom he had met in 1819, for all his protestations of authenticity, the Horse Shoe of his book is fundamentally as "unreal" as Butler; he is a version of the folk hero of the American frontier, and his true origins are to be sought not in biographical fact but in popular tale and legend. Like Mike Brown of *Swallow Barn,* Horse Shoe has been a blacksmith; and his nickname derives both from his trade and from the fact that his small farm in Carolina is bounded by a horseshoe bend of the Catawba River. But his name suggests more: his ironlike physical toughness and his harmonious association with the nonhuman world. The passage in which he is introduced is a clear hint of this fabulous makeup:

> Nature had carved out, in his person, an athlete whom the sculptors might have studied to improve the Hercules. Every lineament of his body indicated strength. His stature was rather above six feet; his chest broad; his limbs sinewy, and remarkable for their symmetry. There seemed to be no useless flesh upon his frame to soften the prominent surface of his muscles; and his ample thigh, as he sat upon horseback, showed the working of its texture at each step, as if part of the animal on which he rode. His was one of those iron forms that might be imagined almost bullet proof. . . . (17-18)

His exploits are equally superhuman. He cannot be kept in captivity, and he is skilled in strategems for slipping out of tight places in his brushes with the enemy. Apprehended along with Butler early in the story, he puts the rough and rascally Tories off guard by joking with them; and, spotting his opportunity, he leaps on his horse and rides off before they even realize what he is contemplating. Fired at, he ducks his head and moves it "from side to side with a view to baffle the aim of the marksmen" (210). And one Tory who manages to chase him finds that he has yet other tricks:

> "In my hurry I left my sword behind me, and, when I came up with him, I laid my hand upon his bridle; but, by some sudden sleight which he has taught his horse, he contrived, somehow or other, to upset me—horse and all—down a bank on the road-side. And, when I lay on the ground sprawling, do you think the jolly runagate didn't rein up and give me a broad laugh, and ask me if he could be of any *sarvice* to me?" (211)

Later, with only the aid of a boy, Horse Shoe manages to convince a British officer and a party of four armed men that he has them surrounded and obtains their surrender. In other exploits he assumes disguises and acts roles so successfully that he even takes in Colonel Tarleton, that notoriously bloody subduer of lower Carolina. No wonder that Horse Shoe crows, in words reminiscent of the ring-tailed roarer's "half-horse, half-alligator" brag, "My name is Brimstone, I am first cousin to Belzebub" (74). He seems to be everywhere, now plotting to pluck Butler from captivity, now disconcerting a party of

Tories, now practicing his night-riding so stealthily that one of his enemies claims to have been the victim of an invisible assailant.

Like the backwoods folk hero, Horse Shoe is chivalric in his attitude toward women but remains a resolute bachelor. " 'Why, sir,' " he bellows to John Ramsay—ribbing Ramsay for his love of Mary Musgrove—" 'if I was a lovable man, haw! haw!—which I'm not—I'll be cursed if I wouldn't spark that little fusee myself' " (314). Nor is Horse Shoe drawn to conventional worship. His attitude toward God is like his feeling for the woods; he lives in harmony with both, trusting in them without any doubts: " 'I'm not much given to religious takings-on, but sometimes a notion comes into my head that looks a little that way, and that is, when God appoints a thing to be done, he gives them that's to do it all the wherewithalls' " (392).

In developing the figure of Horse Shoe, Kennedy was probably influenced by such immediate literary prototypes as Brom Bones of Irving's "The Legend of Sleepy Hollow," Harvey Birch of Cooper's *The Spy,* and Natty Bumppo of the Leather-Stocking Tales. He may also have had in mind the popular legends of Mike Fink, Davy Crockett, and other supermen of the frontier. But the roots of Horse Shoe's character are deep in oral lore. In terms of theme, he represents the spirit of revolt against restraints; he is the shape-shifter and trickster who cannot be contained, the magnificent boy-man whom no antagonist can subdue. Significantly, it is Horse Shoe who keeps the plot in motion; it is he who brings to Mildred the letters from Butler which make her seek out Cornwallis and plead for her husband; it is he who rides with her and protects her on her dangerous quest. And, finally, it is Horse Shoe who effects Butler's rescue and executes summary and bloody judgment on those who have tried to keep him in bondage.

Horse Shoe remains the most engaging—and perhaps the most subtly conceived—of all of Kennedy's creations. He is convincingly real without being at all "realistic." Partly, this appeal is achieved by his curious manner of talking, which is neither a mere imitation of a literary dialect nor an accurate transcription of any actual native speech of the period. Like Natty Bumppo, Horse Shoe is given to yokelish-sounding coinages like "contwistification" and "obstrepolous." But the main trick of his talk is a rhythm and balance which nicely parody the high-flown "correct" rhetoric of his social betters. In an early scene he spars verbally with a man whom he knows to be an enemy and is scornfully snooted: " 'Verily, you are a most comical piece of dulness,' " said the other, in a spirit of raillery. 'In what school did you learn your philosophy, friend? You have been brought up to the wholesome tail of the plough, I should say—an ancient and reputable occupation.' " Horse Shoe, however, knows how to deflate his rival's assumption of superiority:

> "When I observed, just now," replied Robinson, somewhat sternly, "that I couldn't be instigated, I meant to be comprehended as laying down a kind of general doctrine that I was a man not given to quarrels; but still, if I suspicioned a bamboozlement, which I am not far from at this present speaking, if it but come up to the conflagrating of only the tenth part of the wink of an eye, in a project to play me off, fore God, I confess myself to be as weak in the flesh as e'er a rumbunctious fellow you mought meet on the road."

Not surprisingly, the other replies: " 'Friend, I do not understand thy lingo. It has a most clodpolish smack. It is neither grammar, English, nor sense.' " And Horse Shoe, parrying again, at once comes back: " 'Then, you are a damned, onmannerly rascal, and that's grammar, English, and sense, all three' " (69-70).

As the very spirit of rebellion against imposed authority, Horse Shoe combats Tories as naturally as he breathes. But the danger inherent in such a character, Kennedy senses, is that he might remain anarchic—that he might not be content under *any* social order. Kennedy came more and more to distrust the unchecked power of the common man in a democracy, and he betrays this disquiet even in a book designed to celebrate the birth of a republic. Cooper faced a similar conceptual problem with his Natty Bumppo, and he only partly resolved it by sending his hero farther and farther back from the frontiers of developing American civilization. Kennedy's attempted solution was to emphasize the mutually beneficial relationship between upper-class leader and obedient but nonservile squire; if Butler needed the co-operation of Horse Shoe, the scout equally needed to accept the virtues of a native aristocracy. Adolescent America, as prefigured in the manly yet boyish Horse Shoe, had to grow up. Kennedy did not develop this theme of the interaction of upper-class dominance and frontier freedom as exhaustively as did Simms, whose own first romance dealing with the Revolutionary years in the South appeared in this same year of 1835.[11] But Kennedy at least saw the problem as clearly as did his fellow-Southerner: How can there be order without an ordered society? How could the spirit of frontier nonconformity, with its admitted appeal, ever be tamed; and what might be lost if it were? It turned out to be no easier to solve these questions in fiction than in fact.

The Lindsays, Butler, and Horse Shoe carry all the serious meanings of the book; the other characters require, therefore, only a glance. The simple-minded Mary Musgrove supplies the seasoning of sentiment and religiosity which readers of the popular romance expected and which Mildred Lindsay, because of her activist role, could not contribute. Mary's lover, John Ramsay, provides excuse for the tear happily shed for unconsummated passion and personal sacrifice for country. The many villains of the plot—Curry, Habershaw, and the cutthroat bands of Tory renegades—were undoubtedly suggested by the real-life marauders who plundered the South while the British held military control. As characters, though, they are carbons of the dark figures of the Gothic tale and popular melodrama, and it is meaningless to argue that they are more "realistic" simply because they swear and sweat. Certainly their creator would have been puzzled if he had been informed that the Lindsays were any less "true" than were his commoners.

For Kennedy's own concept of the imitation of reality in fiction was entirely of his period. His narrative, so he insisted in the preface to the first edition, was *both* factual and legendary, *both* instructive and entertaining; he had written his book out of these two motives:

> First, because [the events described] intrinsically possess an interest that may amuse the lovers of adventure, and
>
> Second, because they serve to illustrate the temper and character of the War of our Revolution.

But it was the romantic—or imaginative—view of the past which he emphasized:

> As yet, only the political and documentary history of that war has been written. Its romantic or picturesque features have been left for that industrious tribe of chroniclers, of which I hold myself to be an unworthy member, and who have of late, as the public is aware, set about the business in good earnest. It shall go hard with us if we do not soon bring to light every remnant of tradition that the war has left! (11)

Kennedy was indeed concerned with the inner truths of the period, but it was by means of invented characters rather than by a reconstruction of factual events that he inquired after meanings. Perhaps his own attitude is best suggested in a passage between Butler and Horse Shoe near the beginning of the book. Horse Shoe has been recounting an ingenious escape from the hands of Colonel Tarleton; Butler listens wonderingly to the recital and then comments: " 'If I did not know you, Robinson, to be a man of truth, as well as courage, I should scarce believe this tale. If any one, hereafter, should tell your story, he will be accounted a fiction-monger' " (29). Like Butler, we can "scarce believe this tale" as any authentic re-creation of the War of Independence; but, unlike Butler, we need not assume that "fiction" simply equals "a lie." For it is entirely the "fiction" of *Horse-Shoe Robinson*—the thematic conflicts rendered through the imaginary Butler, Horse Shoe, and the Lindsays—which gives to the book whatever reality it may be said to have.

IV *Consumers' Report*

Kennedy had struck a note to which many readers were ready to respond in the mid-1830's, and *Horse-Shoe Robinson* was a fair critical and financial success. Carey & Lea quickly issued a second printing in 1835 and a third in 1836 before the market began to fail. In an "Advertisement to the Third Edition," Kennedy (still signing himself Mark Littleton) thanked his readers for this comforting support and flattered them as "that true-hearted, easily satisfied and generous community who constitute the genuine consumers of works of fiction." He had other reasons for feeling elated. Irving, to whom he had inscribed the book, immediately wrote that he had read it "with great gusto," and he predicted that "Horse Shoe will be a decided favourite with the public."[12] Moreover, Lewis Gaylord Clark, a powerful New York editor, now urged that Kennedy contribute to the *Knickerbocker Magazine* "a tale, or interesting sketches, —and will you, upon your own terms of remuneration?" Closer home, he was pleased to get a shower of congratulatory letters from his fellow townsmen. One James H. Miller, for example, was ready to vouch for the book's authenticity:

> My early reminiscences of Revolutionary characters, scenes & events have been resuscitated in their pristine reality: . . . There is not a character in your work that has not its exact verisimilitude in my recollection. They are all drawn to nature & life. Your own language is chastely & classically elegant & correct, & that of your characters is as true as if it had been taken stenographically at the time.

Such a voucher was heady enough praise, but it was matched by the encomium of Robert Gilmor:

> Much as I was pleased with "Swallow Barn," yet in my opinion "Horse Shoe Robinson" is a superior work, and will I think establish your reputation as an author, not only here, but abroad.— Your story is full of interest which never flags, and is well told.— Your characters are full as well sustained as in your first work, & possess no extravagance or caricature in the delineation, while there is more continuity in it as a tale.—"Horse Shoe" your hero is admirably drawn and is always in action and language the same, without exaggeration, and has the rare merit of being from the very first page before the reader, & mixed up with nearly every transaction.—This keeps your reader's attention always alive & on the alert, and he is not shocked by unexpected & unnatural exhibitions of the man, for by the manner in which you relate his extraordinary exploits they never appear out of character.—The battle of King's mountain is spiritedly told & reminded me of that in [Scott's] Marmion. . . .

Gilmor went on to express his wish that Kennedy had not killed off Philip Lindsay since a Tory should have been given the chance to see the error of his ways; but he liked both the character and the conduct of the spirited Mildred. Finally, he suggested that Kennedy favor his readers with more tales about the Revolution and about the "settlement of our Western Empire" because these were subjects which foreign writers "dare not meddle with."

Newspaper and magazine critics were generally as responsive as these private readers; some even favored Horse Shoe over Natty Bumppo. Poe, now engaged in the editorship of the *Southern Literary Messenger* which Kennedy had helped him to obtain, paid part of his debt with a flattering notice. He found much to admire in Horse Shoe and in the other simple people who, he thought, made the story believable; further, he considered the book notably well written: "We have called the style of Mr. Kennedy a style simple and forcible, and we have no hesitation in calling it, at the same time, richly figurative and poetical." Poe could often be savage in his judgments upon his contemporaries, and it is possible that his own sense of gratitude made him temper his remarks. But he at least sounds sincere in this estimate of Kennedy's career up to this period:

> We have not yet forgotten, nor is it likely we shall very soon forget, the rich simplicity of diction—the manliness of tone—the admirable traits of Virginian manners, and the striking pictures of still life, to be found in Swallow Barn. The spirit of imitation was, however, visible in that book, and, in a great measure, overclouded its rare excellence. This is by no means the case with Mr. Kennedy's new novel. If ever volumes were entitled to be called original—these are so entitled. We have read them from beginning to end with the greatest attention, and feel very little afraid of hazarding our critical reputation, when we assert that they will place Mr. Kennedy at once in the very first rank of American novelists.[13]

Such panegyrics, as surprising as they were welcome to a nonprofessional writer, were often echoed in the other reviews which Kennedy cut from various journals and pasted in his scrapbook. One anonymous Baltimore commentator had the insight to point out that the book mingled "historical truth with the fictitious truth of private sentiment and action," and he opined that it would "have gladdened the heart of great old

Sir Walter."[14] Others took pride in this new evidence that American writers were finally beginning to take full advantage of the subjects provided by national history: "We trust no one will have the hardihood or the stolidity to reiterate, for the next twenty years at least, the trans-Atlantic absurdity that America affords no themes for the poet or the novelist. If any should, we shall but point in silence to the 'Tale of the Tory Ascendancy.'" Another critic concurred:

> Mr. Kennedy is an author whose productions, illustrating as they do, the history and character of his own country, ought to be esteemed and read from patriotic and national considerations. Nothing contributes more effectually to the formation of a just and sensitive pride of country, than the embalming influence of song and romance—and every epic poem or historical novel adds so much not only to the literary fund of the nation, but to that common property which we all have in the renown of past days.

Nearly twenty years later, when Kennedy published a revised edition, his Revolutionary tale still managed to find an appreciative audience. Simms, reviewing it in the *Southern Quarterly Review,* was critical of Kennedy's view of South Carolina's historical role; but he added that he had no wish to detract from the "real merits" of a book which had in so many ways foreshadowed his own later work.[15] But perhaps the most revealing reaction of all is to be found in a letter sent by a Mississippi reader to the editor of a New Orleans paper; in its recognition of the blending of legend and fact, it is a neat summation of what many contemporaries must have found to their liking in Kennedy's story:

> As a work of mixed fiction and historical reminiscences, I have never read its superior. The general plot is new, distinct, powerfully worked out and consistent throughout. The characters are natural—no witches, hobgoblins, or even elfish boys!—no romance inconsistent with real life—no character but what is drawn to the life—well sustained to the end, and, as with Scott, no word or thought offensively obtruding, even in the humble characters which are so accurately natural, . . . to wound the taste of elder persons, or cause a blush on the cheek of the most delicate female, even one just budding into womanhood. . . .

> In Major Butler, the gentleman-hero of the work, we have the real likeness of a country gentleman, or patriot turned soldier, from love of country. . . . It is a true likeness, I doubt not, of the South Carolina Revolutionary Planter and Gentleman. . . . The portrait drawn of Butler is not overwrought by imaginary or romantic qualities, but highly endowed by the bold hand and strong head that created it.
>
> Of the main character, . . . Horse-Shoe Robinson, I should fear to use words strong enough to convey my admiration. He is the beau ideal of a peasant patriot—a patriot in heart—uneducated—who becomes a soldier from convictions of duty to his country, filled with common sense, as well as mother wit. . . . The character is like that of Leather Stocking, created from frontier life, naturally brave—patient—indomitable. . . . [But] I believe that no reader of taste and judgment will give Cooper's frontier character the palm over Kennedy's.
>
> No more interesting times or scenes could have been selected, even out of our revolutionary events, that are full of facts having rather the illusion, at this distance, of romantic fictions, than the reality of life, even in war. . . .[16]

How well Kennedy had succeeded in convincing his readers of the reality of "romantic fiction" about the nation's past such a letter certainly attests.

V *A Whig in Power*

In the years between 1835 and 1838 Kennedy worked on his third and last historical romance, but this was also a period in which he was most active in the councils of the recently formed Whig party. Whiggery had as its original motivating force the widespread opposition to Andrew Jackson on the grounds that he had usurped executive power, but it would continue to be a factor in American politics for some years after "King Andrew the First" left office. Kennedy—who had once been a Jackson man himself—was instrumental in publicizing some of the principles for which his party would stand. Primarily it would claim to be the spokesman for business and commerce, the protector of property rights, the guarantor of a stable economy. Both as propagandist and as an active candidate for public office, Kennedy labored hard to ensure that the positions with which he had become identified would prevail.

In 1837 the local Whigs nominated him for Congress on a strong protectionist platform, and Kennedy suddenly found himself in the middle of a vicious campaign. Old charges were raked up: he had voted for the Potomac canal against the best interests of Baltimore; he had turned down a diplomatic post after having done his best to secure it; he was untrustworthy because he had switched loyalties. Not too surprisingly, in such deeply personal politics, his books were also held against him and made objects of derision. Slurring references were made about his capacities as a creator of fiction, and doubts were cast upon his ability to handle facts. The outcome of this bitterly contested election was Kennedy's defeat, though by a mere two hundred votes.

Several years later he still smarted over the manner in which his services to a national literature had been turned back upon him. Writing in his journal about attacks upon a Virginia politician, Abel P. Upshur, he commented caustically: "[T]o sum up his disqualifications he has committed the crime which the Locos [the Locofocos, a nickname given to a radical faction of Democrats] consider *my* deepest sin, of writing a novel . . . it is called the Partisan Leader—and is altogether political.—I am glad that there is another public man besides myself who can be charged with this atrocity of writing a book.—Paulding wrote half a dozen very bad novels,—but he was a born Loco and so escaped scot free."[17]

Kennedy was wrong in attributing the novel to the author he named here—it was written by another Virginian, Beverley Tucker—but he was correct in assuming that his enemies would always seize upon his authorship of fiction as a vulnerable point. Yet his local popularity was still considerable; and in 1838 he at last won a seat in the House of Representatives in an off-year election, called after the death of the man who had defeated him. The vote polled marked the high point of the Whig forces in Baltimore, and the triumph was undoubtedly a personal victory for Kennedy to savor. He had not been in public office for fifteen years, and his introduction to power on the national stage was to have a potent effect upon the remainder of his literary career. In June, when he made his first speech in the House, he drew attention to himself by his strong defense of the manufacturing interests of the East and his denunciation of the backwardness of Southern states—especially Virginia—in failing to espouse his version of progressivism. Though he experienced political ups and downs, he was an effective representative. At one point during his congressional service he caught the eye of the correspondent of the New York *Times,* who sent to his paper a brief sketch which Kennedy later clipped and pasted in his scrapbook. He was "a striking personage," wrote the reporter, "of fine stature, vigorously though neatly formed, and remarkably careful in his dress and carriage."

> The characteristics of Kennedy's oratory are the perfectness of his composition and the purity of his English, derived from long and close study of the best authors. In this respect, his sensitiveness and taste have refined him, perhaps, too much, and give his productions rather the character of essays, than speeches. . . . His chief peculiarity is, I think, in the use of words not very current in ordinary communication, but with which he has become familiarized by the reading of the better and older writers in our language, and which he has adopted for expressiveness and strength. He has, too, a certain quaint, old-fashioned, majestic, gaunt, yet graceful style, which reminds you of a harmonious blending of the inlaid armour of the Elizabethan age, and the pliant though fanciful habit of the reign of Anne.[18]

These latter words were indeed apt; for, during the summer recess which followed Kennedy's maiden speech, he devoted himself to the completion of a story which was "quaint," "old-fashioned," and about a period not too far removed from the Elizabethan age. This book, which he called *Rob of the Bowl,* was set in the province of Maryland in the latter part of the seventeenth century, and it would prove to be his most ambitious foray into historical fiction. In his search for fresh materials through which he hoped to enrich the average American's knowledge of his varied past, Kennedy had now turned from the Virginia of his mother's forebears to the state which he could claim as his own. *Rob of the Bowl* was clearly an attempt to try his hand at a reconstruction which demanded even more imaginative insight, and he probably envisaged it as the first of a series of colonial romances. But after its publication his career as a man of affairs closed in upon him, and *Rob* was the last important work of literature which he would offer to the public that had so enthusiastically received his first two books.[19]

CHAPTER 4

Rob of the Bowl: The Cavalier Ethic

I *The Old Society*

SPURRED ON BY THE POPULARITY of *Horse-Shoe Robinson,* Kennedy had begun late in September of 1835 to work out the idea for a new historical romance. He might easily, like Simms, have gone on combing the records of the Revolution for usable episodes; but, continuing his march backward into the past, Kennedy at once hit upon colonial Maryland as his setting. The specific subject matter, however, he found difficult to pin down. In the earliest journal entry concerning his plan, he could suggest only an approximate place and time:

> Began today to model out a new book. I have not yet fixed on the story, but mean to put it upon the Chesapeake—just before the revolution about 1774, perhaps.—To introduce Billy of the Bowl, the pirate or buccaneer & smuggler, Cocklescraft[,] a family of old maids on the Eastern Shore [of Maryland] the Lacklands—Gilmore's Parson who according to the autograph letter in Gilmore's possession had to read the service with his pistols on his desk—&c. &c.[1]

This notation indicates that Kennedy intended from the outset to compose an even freer type of romance, one in which actual historical events would be made quite subordinate to legend, anecdote, and invented story. Certainly the first of the numerous pages of manuscript notes recording various versions and stages of his book supports this impression:

> I propose to write a tale partly grave and partly comic descriptive of the manners of the old society upon the Chesapeake, at a period before the establishment of the government when the people still retained the subordination and respect of the old system of things before the revolution. I think I shall lay the scene on the bay shore, below Patuxent in Charles or St. Mary's [counties].
>
> I wish to describe a stiff old campaigner of the war with an only daughter.—a neighbouring family consisting of a number of old maids living with a widowed sister and her children. Both families to be of good estate and belonging to the best class of society.—The adventures of the story may be given to a son of the campaigner. I may introduce watermen, pirates &c. on the Chesapeake. *Billy of the bowl* may figure as a part of my machinery.
>
> The whole tale to be entirely fictitious. I would introduce the indians of the time—the feuds of the Catholics & Protestants in Maryland. The spirit of the society at Annapolis—The fighting clergyman for which see Mr. Gilmor's letter. Date the story about the period of that letter.[2]

A few succeeding random sentences contain admonitions to himself to procure and read a standard history of Maryland and make a visit to the proposed scene of the tale. The entry then continues:

> Remember the story of the blood spots on the floor at Denton.—and the strange echo from a bridge, giving a house the reputation of being haunted.
>
> Billy of the Bowl might be described as an old man who in early life had a son towards whom he had a strong aversion—He has lost his legs by frost—is dissolute, knavish and shrewd—insensible to the ordinary feelings of a parent—fond of low company. . . .[3]

These rather jumbled jottings are hazy on the possibilities of narrative development, and it is likely that at the date of their writing Kennedy could not find the leisure to follow them through. A second set of notes—probably set down some time later than the preceding—begins to suggest the structure which he would finally adopt:

> I propose to write a tale descriptive of American, or rather Maryland manners and scenery previous to the revolution, [the incidents of which shall be entirely fictitious without reference to any passage of history].[4] The scene shall be laid upon the Chesapeake between Annapolis and Patuxent or perhaps as low as St. Marys, and shall shift occasionally to the Eastern Shore.
>
> We have here in Maryland some tradition of buccaneers and smugglers frequenting the Chesapeake and I shall introduce this kind of agency into my story. I have heard also of a little fellow who had lost his legs and who consequently was strapped in a huge wooden bowl and I think was called Billy of the Bowl. This worthy flourished, it strikes me, during the Revolutionary war and was connected with some exploit of capturing a small tender which got aground somewhere along the bay shore. I shall turn him to some account by representing a personage under the same nick name who shall move about in his wooden trencher with short crutches, and I will endow him with some faculty of horsemanship and sometimes describe him in this guise mounted, and with his bowl hung like a shield at his back. He shall be saucy, sarcastic, malicious, envious &c. I think there is a cripple who hobbles in a bowl in Victor Hugo's Hunchback. . . .
>
> My buccaneer I shall call Cocklescraft and make him a good sailor, a handsome fellow, very brave, wild, dissolute, comic &c. He shall pretend to some skill in the black art and practise it to make weak people afraid of him. But he shall be rather a favourite with the watermen and others on the bay side on account of his free trading. I mean to have a haunted house for the use of him and his gang. In this house I shall introduce the ordinary terrors which are said to have belonged to more than one mansion in this state—such as confusion amongst the moveables at night &c. and I shall also give it the addition of an echo which, as I once heard, made a house near Williamsburg an object of especial abhorrence—the echo of horses or wagons passing over a bridge not far off, reverberated so singularly in the house as long to defy all endeavours to explain it, and cause a most superstitious dread in the vicinity. . . .

A few traces of this rusty "supernatural" machinery—reminiscent of the popular Gothic romances and tales of Irving like "The Legend of Sleepy Hollow" and "The Spectre Bridegroom"—were allowed to remain in the published text. Kennedy appears to have been uneasy, however, about being lured into too much fanciful embroidery; for in a note immediately following this passage, he posits a frame device to create an air of verisimilitude: "There should be an introduction to the story which might purport to be Fragments from the Journal of some fictitious person. The introduction should tell the tale of which the following is an outline. . . ." This scaffolding—which he had already utilized in *Swallow Barn* and in the first edition of *Horse-Shoe Robinson*—was eventually thrown out; but the idea allowed Kennedy to carry on with a fully developed sketch of the early career in England of Billy of the Bowl (later to be rechristened Rob). To this introduction he then added some brief plot summaries, a mass of historical notes, and drafts of several complete chapters; the date of the action, put down tentatively as 1704, was finally fixed as 1681.

But, in spite of this growing pile of manuscript materials, Kennedy found that finishing his book was extraordinarily difficult. His service to the Whig party was now demanding much of his time; and it was not until the spring of 1838 that he felt he had accomplished enough to warrant approaching his Philadelphia publishers with news of his progress. On April 5, 1838, Carey & Lea replied to his note that they were pleased to hear he was again writing, since they had "little doubt as to the merit of any romance you might produce." They were wary, however, about appearing enthusiastic and lamented that the publishing business was currently in a decline. What, they asked, would Kennedy charge for permission to print an edition of three thousand copies? Yet they still sounded dubious: "What do you propose to call it? Where is the scene laid & at what time? What will be the size of it? Do you remember that monster Robinson? His vastness was better calculated for fighting than profit. We hope this will be in two genteel vols or as a latinist would say gracilis—at the same time not too slender."[5]

Kennedy responded with reassurances that he would remember their interests, but the publishers continued their hand-wringing: "We paid you for Horse Shoe $1200 for 3000 copies. Then the demand for books was much greater particularly for works of the imagination." Now, alas, their sales had dropped badly in the South and West, and they could promise only to print four thousand copies as a trial and assure the author a flat sum of $1,600. Apparently Kennedy was piqued by Carey & Lea's tone and tried elsewhere, for in this same month he received a letter from Harper & Brothers offering to pay him $1,200 for one edition of three thousand or, alternatively, to stereotype the plates and share the profits from all sales on a fifty-fifty basis. At this stage Kennedy, tied up with his duties in the House of Representatives, turned negotiations over to his father-in-law; and Gray finally settled with Carey & Lea, agreeing on $1,850 in remuneration for an edition of four thousand—with twenty-five copies given to the author.

What neither Kennedy nor his father-in-law told the publishers, however, was that the book was still far from completion. He had now been working on it at random intervals for more than two years, but he had not been able to develop his drafts into a finished text. From July through October, while Congress was in recess, he retired to Virginia, took a water cure for his constantly annoying eczema, and gave considerable time to his recalcitrant literary materials. By September he was reporting to his wife: "I make good from ten to twelve pages of Rob every day and work very much to my satisfaction—calculating according to my contract that my labour, of about three hours, stands me from eighteen to twenty dollars daily. If I can contrive to keep this up in a few more books I shall do very well."[6] Though this vision of "a few more books" would prove to be delusory, Kennedy at least completed his tale of colonial Maryland. On December 14—more than three years after he had jotted down his first journal entry—his publishers (now operating under the name of Lea & Blanchard) finally informed him that the romance would be issued the next day.

II *St. Mary's City*

Because *Rob of the Bowl,* subtitled *A Legend of St. Inigoe's,* is the least known and the most difficult to obtain of Kennedy's three works of fiction, a sketch of its main action will be useful before I consider the explicit and implicit meanings of the text.[7] As in *Horse-Shoe Robinson,* Kennedy opens the book with a leisurely, nostalgic chapter of scene painting. The setting is the "ancient" capital of Maryland, the small town of St. Mary's, which once stood on the lower western shore of Chesapeake Bay. Now the site is desolate, and only a few pathetic ruins remain to remind the visitor of this nearly forgotten period of American history. At the time of the story, though—autumn of the year 1681—St. Mary's was a bustling little community; it boasted a State House, a fort and a jail, the large house occupied by the Lord Proprietary, and a tavern. Chapters II and III, which are set in the fort, are rather static exposition. Kennedy introduces Captain Jasper Dauntrees, an old campaigner of the English and Continental wars, who now commands the defenses of the port. Modeled on Falstaff, with a tempering dash of other nobler Shakespearean heroes, Dauntrees is a toper and wit but also a ready swordsman.

As the scene begins, he is savoring a drinking bout with two regular cronies: Garret Weasel, publican of the "Crow and Archer," and Arnold de la Grange, a forester in the service of the Lord Proprietary. Their bibulous gossip gives the backgrounds of the chief plot lines. Charles Calvert, Lord Baltimore (the Proprietary), is currently beset by internal quarrels. A Catholic, he has tried to abide by the statute of religious freedom instituted by the founders of the province, but dissident Protestants have rebelled against his rule and intrigued against his coreligionists. Talk of the Proprietary now leads to speculation about the identity of his secretary, a handsome, moody young man called Albert Verheyden. Dauntrees, on cue, rehearses what he knows of Verheyden's origins: he had been born in Yorkshire to the wife of one Major William Weatherby; the major, suspicious of the attentions paid to his wife by a neighbor named Sir George Alwin, had stabbed Alwin to death and then fled the country. His wife, following the birth of Albert, had returned to her native Holland; there the boy was taken in charge by Jesuits and given an excellent schooling. Lord Baltimore, on a visit to Antwerp, had seen the youth by chance and had taken him into his own service. This is all the story that

Dauntrees knows, for the fate of Albert's father is left a mystery which Kennedy saves for resolution late in the story.

The conversation of Dauntrees and his companions turns also on the equally mysterious Robert Swale—locally known as Trencher Rob or Rob of the Bowl because, having lost his legs, he gets about by strapping himself in a wooden, bowl-like contraption. Rob, an ill-tempered, sarcastic man, is believed to be in league with smugglers, especially with Richard Cocklescraft, master of a ship which is due soon in port; and Garret Weasel is teased because of the well-founded suspicion that he obtains some of his wines and liquors through dealings with these men.

With this exposition cleared away, Kennedy moves in Chapter IV to the hall of Lord Baltimore, where the Proprietary queries Dauntrees about reports of apparently supernatural happenings at a fisherman's house on the beach at nearby St. Jerome's; he suspects that the leaders of his Protestant enemies, John Coode and Josias Fendall, may be using it for some underhanded purpose. But Dauntrees knows the story of this place: in it a certain Paul Kelpy had murdered his family and then committed suicide; now called "the Wizard's Chapel," it is shunned as the scene of hellish lights and weird apparitions. A visit to the chapel, made at the Proprietary's request by Dauntrees, de la Grange, Weasel, and an Indian named Pamesack, confirms these rumors; they discover that whatever inhabits it does not want to be investigated since they are fired upon. The house is, of course, the headquarters and warehouse for the gang of smugglers.

Meanwhile, Lord Baltimore has summoned his council members to inform them that letters from London have ordered that all the offices of the province must be transferred immediately from their Catholic holders to members of the Church of England party. One of these proscribed officials is Anthony Warden, collector of the port, and father of the beautiful Blanche, who is destined to be the heroine. As every reader of romance could guess, Albert Verheyden is in love with Blanche, and she returns his love. Now a new plot complication begins to develop with the arrival in port of Cocklescraft, the salty, swashbuckling smuggler who commands the ship *Olive*

Branch. Invited to a birthday party given to honor Blanche, he immediately lusts after her and asks the astounded Anthony Warden for permission to woo her. His violent rebuff convinces Cocklescraft that she must favor Albert, and a duel ensues between the two rivals. Coached by Dauntrees, the pallid and reserved Albert unexpectedly proves the victor, though he is chided by his patron for such illegal brawling. Cocklescraft, vowing to avenge himself on the whole leader class, secretly joins the Protestant faction.

Kennedy now divides the remaining actions of the book between those which have some claim to historicity and those which are purely imaginary. During a public trial of arms between a man who is supported by the Protestant faction and another who is the favorite of the Catholics, the simmering religious quarrel explodes into a riot which the authorities are required to use force to put down. With this temporary check to the Protestants and the jailing of their leaders, Kennedy leaves history to return to his invented characters. Albert Verheyden, investigating for Lord Baltimore a report that Indians plan to attack the settlement from the north, wanders by chance into the Wizard's Chapel and falls asleep. Here he is discovered by Rob of the Bowl, who is struck with terror by his appearance and by the miniature of a woman's face which he wears. In an aside, Rob now reveals himself as the William Weatherby whose story Dauntrees had related; and, when Cocklescraft enters and delightedly takes his old rival prisoner, Rob arranges for Albert's escape.

Balked, the furious Cocklescraft next raids the home of the Wardens and abducts Blanche, planning to take her with him to sea. But Rob has foiled Cocklescraft a second time; he has managed to have the *Olive Branch* hidden away, and the fast-following Dauntrees and Albert capture him before harm can come to Blanche. In a final scene Rob, fatally wounded by Cocklescraft, acknowledges Albert as his son and receives his forgiveness; the pirate, in the confusion which follows his act of revenge upon Rob, breaks loose, gets to his ship, and sails off. This escape, the only real surprise of the book, was probably dictated by Kennedy's intention to employ him in a sequel. Even so, he can close the book on a happy note with the marriage of Albert and Blanche, with the reversion of Rob's considerable wealth to his son, and with a few random historical notes about the fate of the conspirators against Lord Baltimore.

Thus reduced to brief summation, *Rob of the Bowl* sounds like a rather foolish story, and it cannot be denied that its melodrama and sentimentality may well strike the present-day reader as adolescent. To a great extent Kennedy's varied source materials are responsible for the unevenness of effect. He had wanted to write accurately of the colonial period; he had saturated himself in the records of early St. Mary's, which he borrowed from the state librarian; and he had taken some pains in searching for authentic details like proper names.[8] But, while the story has this sort of minor validity as an exposition of the epoch of the clashes between Catholics and Protestants, its value as genuine record is undercut by the heavy reliance on extraneous literary models. Once again, *Rob* reminds us that the historical romance is never historical, that its true value resides in the ways in which the author views the past from his own vantage-point.

As the reader sees for himself, several of the main characters are derived directly from the Elizabethan and Jacobean drama, and whatever life they possess depends more upon our associating them with their originals than upon Kennedy's own skill as a creator. The tavern scenes, for example, are an attempt to transport Falstaff's Boar's-Head Tavern to a New-World setting, with Weasel's wife taking the role of a thoroughly laundered Mistresss Quickly. Kennedy composes this archaic dialogue with evident relish, but he is still a pale imitator. One long quotation suffices to give the flavor of such episodes. In Chapter X we find Dauntrees planning to persuade Mistress Weasel to allow her husband to accompany him on the expedition to the Wizard's Chapel. This colloquy then ensues:

> "Welcome, dame," [Dauntrees] said, without rising from his seat, at the same time offering his hand, which was readily accepted by the landlady.—"By St. Gregory and St. Michael both, a more buxom and tidy piece of flesh and blood hath never sailed between the two headlands of Potomac, than thou art! You are for a junketing, Mistress Dorothy; you are tricked out like a queen this evening! I have never seen you in your new

> suit before. You are as gay as a marygold: and I wear your colors, thou laughing mother of mischief! Green is the livery of your true knight. Has your good man, honest Garret, come home yet, dame?"
>
> "What would you with my husband, Master Baldpate! There is no good in the wind when you throw yourself into the big chair of this parlor."
>
> "In truth, dame, I only came to make a short night of it with you and your worthy spouse. Do not show your white teeth at me, hussy,—you are too old to bite. Tell Matty to spread supper for me in this parlor. Arnold and Pamesack will partake with me; and if the veritable and most authentic head of this house—I mean yourself, mistress—have no need of Garret, I would entreat to have him in company. By the hand of thy soldier, Mistress Dorothy! I am glad to see you thrive so in your calling. You will spare me Garret, dame? Come, I know you have not learnt how to refuse me a boon."
>
> "You are a saucy Jack, Captain," replied the dame. "I know you of old: you would have a rouse with that thriftless babe, my husband. You sent him reeling home only last night. How can you look me in the face, knowing him, as you do, for a most shallow vessel, Captain Dauntrees?"
>
> "Fie on thee, dame! You disgrace your own flesh and blood by such a speech. Did you not choose him for his qualities?—ay, and with all circumspection, as a woman of experience. You had two husbands before Garret, and when you took him for a third, it was not in ignorance of the sex. . . ." (88-89)

The scene ends with Dauntrees' playing a practical joke on Mistress Weasel which allows Garret to escape for the adventure.

Kennedy's third chief source—in addition to historical record and the older English drama—was popular Gothic and sentimental fiction; and it is in these respects that his book is most vulnerable. The mystery of Albert's origins and the true identity of Rob of the Bowl are stock devices of a fairly low order of invention. Kate of Warrington, an old hag who waits on Rob, and Cocklescraft are equally derivative figures; and the Wizard's Chapel, though suggested by local legends which Kennedy had collected, is in effect a gratuitous Gothic touch. Such hackneyed materials, however much they lured a contemporary audience, may only jar the modern reader of the book. But—as in *Swallow Barn* and *Horse-Shoe Robinson*—the explicit story, I believe, is far less important than its implicit meanings. What it finally reveals is not the image of seventeenth-century Maryland but a projected view of nineteenth-century America.

III *The Uncommon Man*

Kennedy himself could not have agreed with this judgment. He had, after all, undertaken far more research than the average romancer deemed necessary: he had combed through documents; he had woven actual quotations into his text; he had even visited the site of St. Mary's and the surrounding countryside. As he boasted in his preface, he had "aimed to perform his task with historical fidelity." And the conclusion of this preface emphasizes that the "war of intolerance" had been his principal concern:

> If he has set in harsher lights than may be deemed charitable some of the actors in these scenes, or portrayed in lineaments of disparagement or extenuation, beyond their deserts, the partisans on either side in that war of intolerance which disfigured the epoch of this tale, it was apart from his purpose. As a native of the state, he feels a prompt sensibility to the fame of her Catholic founders, and, though differing from them in his faith, cherishes the remembrance of their noble endeavors to establish religious freedom, with the affection due to what he believes the most wisely planned and honestly executed scheme of society which at that era, at least, was to be found in the annals of mankind. In the temper inspired by this sentiment, these volumes have been given to the public, and are now respectfully inscribed to THE STATE OF MARYLAND, by one who takes the deepest interest in whatever concerns her present happiness or ancient renown. (5-6)

Kennedy's clearly announced purpose, then, was patriotic service: the native son would give the touch of his vivifying genius to records which had long been forgotten and to an era which seemed as remote as Greece and Rome to the inhabitants of the bustling, modern mercantile state. As late as 1854, when *Rob of the Bowl* was reissued for the first time, he was still proclaiming his fidelity to fact in a preface written for, but not used in, this new edition:

> . . . I think I may claim for my work, notwithstanding its air of romance, that it is as yet the only sketch which has given a picture of the events of that time. It might amuse the reader if I were to open to his inspection the large groundwork of actual history upon which the superstructure of fiction is built—but that would be a more appropriate task for a separate essay than a preface to the tale, and I therefore abandon it for the present, looking in some other form to resuscitate this forgotten chapter of history. It is sufficient for me to say that the vexations to which Charles Lord Baltimore—a most worthy and exemplary gentleman, and a most conscientious and excellent governor—was exposed in the course of a long and difficult administration, are as faithfully developed in this romance as they could be in any history I might write; that the principal personages who surrounded him in that period of trial are, for the most part, real actors in the events in connection with which they are presented, and that the picture I have given, of the time[,] manners, temper and purposes of those who figured in it, making due allowance for the necessary privilege of romance, is a faithful embodiment of my own view of actual historical realities, in the true exhibition of which I am conscious no more lively or truthful representation can be given than through this medium of fiction. Indeed, I would say that in this dramatic form of exposition, when well accomplished, we have the highest and best instrumentality for painting the truth.[9]

Kennedy's claims, nevertheless, must be heavily discounted. He deemed popular legend as important to his purposes as any written record; he shifted characters and events from other times and places to the milieu of his story; he created dialogue in which he drew from sources which had nothing to do with late seventeenth-century Maryland; he turned the primitiveness of the actual colonial setting into a picturesque stage backdrop. Moreover, it is notable that the historical episodes which he found entered in the archives do *not* make up the major portion of his book. The fear of Indian attack, for example, haunted the community; and in early 1681 the settlers were panicked by a report of a planned raid brought to them by a traveler from New York and a "Dutch doctor." Kennedy, however, develops the "Dutch doctor" as a figure of fun, and the Indian threat is buried in the comedy and soon largely forgotten.[10] It is true that he treats the struggle for dominance between Catholics and Protestants much more fully, but even this central subject is integrally linked with the entirely fictitious events of which the book is chiefly composed. Why, then, did Kennedy claim that his book was a faithful re-creation? In what way could it better serve its readers than a verbatim transcription of the genuine archives?

As his unpublished preface flatly states, Kennedy's defense was embodied in that paradoxical phrase, "the truth of fiction." Like other contemporaneous historical romancers, he argued that the unadorned factual record was never exciting enough; it could not stimulate the imaginations of a people who more than half believed what European critics were tiresomely telling them—that they lacked any past worth memorializing. To reshape American history into colorful adventure, then, was not to falsify it but to bring it to life. Straightforward history, moreover, was morally neutral, as historical fiction certainly was not. The conscientious romancer was concerned with instruction as well as with entertainment; he felt that the past contained lessons which only the imaginative writer could reveal and pass on to the present day. What such an attitude led to, of course, was not history but fantasy—not a record recounted but a myth invented. As Kennedy admitted, *Rob of the Bowl* represented *his* own view of the realities of the past which could be truthfully celebrated only through the medium of fiction. But what was that view? The material that finally remains of interest in his book is the way in which, from the vantage-point of the 1830's, he read the inner meanings of the chronicle of a long-dead age.

Rob of the Bowl advances the general proposition that the leaders in the founding of Maryland were "Cavaliers"—gentlemen of good birth, honor, bravery, tolerance. They were the sons of the best English stock of a golden era; they had brought to the New World some of the glory of the age of Elizabeth and the gallantry of the wars for the King. Significantly, Kennedy's exemplar of the Cavalier spirit is not the historical Lord Baltimore or any of the Calvert clan; it is the entirely fictional Captain Jasper Dauntrees. Superficially, Dauntrees is a Falstaff-figure; but recollection of *Swallow Barn* suggests that his real prototype is the soldier-hero whom Littleton apostrophizes, Captain John Smith. The passage in which Dauntrees is introduced draws an obvious parallel between their wide-ranging martial careers:

> This worthy had been bred up to the science of arms from early youth, and had seen many varieties of service,—first, in the civil wars in which he took the field with the royal army, a staunch cavalier,—and afterwards, with a more doubtful complexion of loyalty, when he enlisted with Monk in Scotland, and followed his banner to London in the notable exploit of the Restoration. Yielding to the bent of that humor which the times engendered, and in imitation of many a hungry and peace-despising gallant of his day, he repaired to the continent, where, after various fortunes, he found himself in the train of Turenne and hard at loggerheads with the Prince of Orange, in which passage of his life he enjoyed the soldierly gratification of lending a hand to the famous ravage of the Palatinate. (17)

Now Dauntrees had come to Maryland "to gather for his old age that harvest of wealth and ease which the common report promised to all who set foot upon the golden shores of the Indies—Maryland, in vulgar belief, being a part of this land of wonders." He had not picked up gold in the streets, but he had found what had proved more valuable and enduring: a pleasant climate, a job which gave him position without too much exertion, a good friend in the Lord Proprietary, and a few sportive drinking companions. Thus a flower of European soldiery—with all the noble virtues and with a few humanizing vices—has taken root in New World soil. As a leader, Dauntrees does not have the stiffness of Major Arthur Butler of *Horse-Shoe Robinson,* and he can frequent the tavern without losing status. In this age when, as Kennedy had written in his early notes, "the people still retained the subordination and respect of the old system of things," he can take pride in his rank without appearing to be a prig; his character, we are told, revealed

> a compound, not unfrequent in the civil wars of that period, of the precisian and ruffler—the cavalier and economist. In the affairs of life . . . he was worldly-wise, sagaciously provident, as an old soldier, of whatever advantages his condition might casually supply; in words, he was, indifferently, according to the occasion, a moralist or hot-brained reveller—sometimes affecting the courtier along with the martialist, and mixing up the saws of peaceful thrift with the patter of the campaigns. (19)

Though their ranks are entirely different, Dauntrees serves Lord Baltimore much as Horse Shoe does Major Butler; it is he who goes on expeditions, conducts duels, uncovers plots, reunites the lovers, punishes the villains. A Catholic like his patron, he worships in a simple and unsophisticated manner; and he is tolerant of all: the Protestant rebels like Fendall and Coode must be quelled not because of their religion but because of their desire to undermine the authority of the Proprietary. As Kennedy sees him, Dauntrees is the symbol of the founding fathers' active spirit; a soldier of unshakeable honor, he is not self-seeking but dedicated to the growth of the colony. In short, he is a man whom the Old World has trained to be a fit leader of the New.

Albert Verheyden, who is the sentimental hero of the book, does not fare so well as a created character. He is a gentler Cavalier than Dauntrees and represents the intellectual rather than the activist virtues. Kennedy dwells upon this side of his character as he first describes him:

> His face, distinguished by a decided outline of beauty, wore a thoughtful expression, which was scarcely overcome by the flash of a black and brilliant eye. A complexion pale, and even feminine, betokened studious habits. His dress, remarkable for its neatness, denoted a becoming pride of appearance in the wearer. It told of the Low Countries. A well-fitted doublet and hose, of a grave color, were partially concealed by a short camlet [silk and wool] cloak of Vandyke brown. A black cap and feather, a profusion of dark hair hanging in curls towards the shoulders, and a falling band or collar of lace, left it unquestionable that the individual I have sketched was of gentle nurture, and associated with persons of rank. (32)

Albert's accomplishments are those of the Renaissance courtier, upon whom Kennedy evidently modeled him. He is a good swordsman, a passable singer and lute player, a reader of courtly romances, an excellent follower, and a potential leader. In *Swallow Barn* Kennedy had treated such a chivalric ideal with some amusement in several of the passages between Ned Hazard and Bel Tracy. But in Albert he presents the genuine article; and, though he is unconvincingly portrayed, he is seriously intended. Albert is the Genteel Gentleman who balances off Dauntrees, and he is rewarded with Ideal Womanhood in the person of Blanche Warden.

Through such invented characters as Dauntrees and Verheyden—and to a lesser extent through such historical personages as Lord Baltimore and Colonel Talbot—Kennedy is suggesting prototypes against which the present ought to measure itself. Embodied here, too, is his retort to those critics who had sneered at America's plebeian origins: once there were Cavaliers, as well as Puritans, on our shores. Kennedy's general intention in mythicizing these figures is clear enough, but his treatment of the religious element is at first glance puzzling. These heroes are all staunch Catholics; and, though officially committed to free worship for Christians, they patently scorn outsiders like Josias Fendall. Why, then, did Kennedy (himself a Protestant) portray Catholicism in such a sympathetic manner? The obvious answer is that he was a tolerant man and that he took pride in Maryland's efforts on behalf of religious liberty. But the Roman Church, as he viewed it, also offered possibilities for the enrichment of his themes. It was an exotic in the American woods: it had an ancient ritual; it encouraged decoration and was a patron of the arts (even Rob owns a small painting by no less a master than Salvator Rosa!); it was aristocratic, worldly, sophisticated—and a careful conservator. Kennedy could thus celebrate antiquity, stability, and culture as an integral part of the colonial heritage; little St. Mary's was an outpost of Rome and London.

In its implied attitude toward leaders and commoners, *Rob of the Bowl* moved a step beyond even *Horse-Shoe Robinson*. By 1838 Kennedy had observed the brawling of politicians at the national level, and he was becoming appalled by the course which a bustling, prospering, and utilitarian America had embarked upon. Within a year he would be engaged upon the outspokenly anti-Jacksonian satire which he called *Quodlibet;* here, by way of anticipation, he dramatizes a similar distrust of leveling. *Rob* is Kennedy's criticism of the present by historical contrast; it is also the medium for his inquiry after lasting values in an earlier America—values by which his countrymen might gauge their own beliefs and aspirations. In retrospect, it is reasonable to assume that he finally chose the 1680's because the documentary record showed that, like his own period, this era was a time of challenge to an older order. "New men" like the Fendalls and Coode had been trying to wrest away the power vested in the person of Lord Baltimore; and the leaders had been forced to respond. As the story shows, the struggle involved not only religious differences but also the Proprietary's right to appoint local officials. Kennedy comments that Lord Baltimore was not entirely surprised by the orders from London which instructed him to transfer power to the Church of England party; he knew that despite the continued friendship of the monarch his religious and political enemies would find a way to influence their own supporters in England. But the charges brought against him he deemed unfair and underhanded:

> The mandate was especially harsh in reference to the Proprietary, first because it was untrue that he had ever recognized the difference of religious opinion in his appointments, but on the contrary had conferred office indiscriminately in strict and faithful accordance with the fundamental principle of toleration upon which his government was founded; and, secondly, because it would bear with pointed injustice upon some of his nearest and most devoted friends—his uncle the chancellor, the whole of his council, and, above all others in whose welfare he took an interest, upon the collector of the port of St. Mary's, Anthony Warden, an old inhabitant of the province, endeared to the Proprietary—and indeed to all his fellow-burgesses—by long friendship and tried fidelity. What rendered it more grating to the feelings of the Proprietary in this instance, was that the collectorship had already been singled out as a prize to be played for by that faction which had created the late disturbances in the province. It was known that Coode had set

> his eyes upon this lure, and gloated upon it with the gaze of a serpent. The emoluments of the post were something considerable, and its importance was increased by the influence it was supposed to confer on the incumbent, as a person of weight and consequence in the town. (49-50)

Yet, in spite of his forebodings, the Proprietary reacts to this cabal against him with the sorrow of one who has only just discovered that the spoils system controls the deeds of men of no idealism:

> "Am I to be schooled in my duty by rapacious malcontents, and to be driven to put away my trustiest friends, to make room for such thirsty leeches and coarse rufflers as John Coode? The argument is, that here, in what my father would have made a peaceful contented land, planted by him and the brothers of his faith,—with the kindest, best, and most endeared supporters of that faith by my side—worthy men, earnest and zealous to do their duty—they and their children true to every Christian precept—men who have won a home by valor and patient, wise endurance—they must all be disenfranchised, as not trustworthy even for the meanest office, and give their places to brawlers, vaporing bullies and factious stirrers-up of discord—and that, too, in the name of religion! . . ." (50-51)

Lord Baltimore's argument is direct enough: to give in without a struggle is to betray idealism under the pressure of crass "bullies" unfit for rule and incapable of using the profits of their offices for the satisfaction of anything beyond personal greed. The attraction to the conspirators' cause of Cocklescraft—a smuggler and pirate—is a symbolic act which underlines Kennedy's own attitude toward those who would depose traditional leadership and deny the principle of hereditary property rights. And so, as an object lesson, he resolves the factional struggle by detailing the defeat of the Protestant party and emphasizing the magnanimous behavior of Lord Baltimore in dealing with his quondam enemies.

Kennedy's deep-rooted belief in the primacy of property unhappily drives him, in those sections of the book which relate to the title character, to a conclusion of dubious morality. Rob, though originally a gentleman, had murdered a neighbor, fled from England, left his wife and son without support. According to the generally accepted account, he had been cast upon the shores of the New World after a shipwreck and lost his legs as the aftereffect of frostbite. But Rob has expected no sympathy from the colonists and will accept none. He has turned bitterly against humanity and lives as a recluse, but he manages nevertheless to pile up considerable wealth through his partnership with the smugglers. His death at the hands of Cocklescraft, whom he has twice betrayed, is an entirely fitting end; and his dying words to Albert Verheyden and Albert's forgiveness of his father are the purest bathos. But his story does not end here; he leaves Albert a fair-sized fortune, and Kennedy is patently uneasy about allowing his hero to accept riches proper to his station when they come from a tainted source:

> The worldly wise will be pleased, perhaps, to learn that, after some most liberal appropriations to charitable uses, by way of purification of the more than doubtful uncleanness of the Cripple's wealth, Albert fell heir to no small hoard; and this gear, as it was generously distributed in acts of hospitality and bounty to the poor, we would fain hope the straitest casuist will allow, was not unjustly taken by the Secretary. . . . (430)

This sort of reward is to be expected in a purely romantic tale, but it unpleasantly echoes Lord Baltimore's juster claims to hereditary property rights and forces Kennedy to compromise his serious themes.

In general, however, the "Cavalier" ethic prevails throughout *Rob of the Bowl.* We are meant to admire power and position in the family of the Calverts, the spirit of tolerance among the Catholics, the graceful manners of the gentleman, the bravery and Renaissance lustiness of a Dauntrees, and the courage exhibited by colonists who must face enemies within and without. It is an age to which Kennedy was emotionally drawn, and it is one toward which he wishes the present to look back with pride. And yet his opening chapter of historical reminiscence and topographical description betrays the same sort of ambivalence which characterized his two earlier books. Once this land was new; its inhabitants lived both in anxiety and hope in this morning of the New World. It was "a secure and prosperous habitation"; the "great ocean forest" had already receded a hundred miles westward; and the Indians—though still a menace—had their own domain. But today, a nostalgic Kennedy mourns in a burst of bravura rhetoric:

> They are gone! Like shadows have these men of might sunk on the earth. They, their game, their wigwams, their monuments, their primeval forests,—yea, even their graves, have flitted away in this spectral flight. Saxon and Norman, bluff Briton and heavy Suabian inherit the land. And in its turn, well-a-day! our pragmatical little city hath departed. Not all its infant glory, nor its manhood's bustle, its walls, gardens and bowers,—its warm housekeeping, its gossiping burghers, its politics and its factions,—not even its prolific dames and gamesome urchins could keep it in the upper air until this our day. . . . (12-13)

Once it was, but now it is gone. Kennedy's dilemma is embodied in the ways in which this sentence can be construed. Once it was, but now it is *gone*: the progress in which he believed and to which he had dedicated his political life had obliterated these traces of early beginnings. Now it is gone, but once it *was*: the past can again have life and meaning when rendered into a romance through which the present can recall the old virtues. How far had America advanced by the fourth decade of the nineteenth century! And how much of his noble heritage had the Jacksonian "common man" forgotten!

IV *A Hope Rebuffed*

Kennedy had hoped that *Rob of the Bowl* would have a popular and critical acclaim comparable to that of *Horse-Shoe Robinson,* and so—obviously—had his publishers. But only three months after its appearance Lea & Blanchard were writing to him: "As to a new edition of 'Rob' we are sorry to say there is no probability of it. The book has not by any means succeeded to our expectations."[11] It was not that the tale was badly reviewed; rather, it was hardly noticed at all, and Kennedy pasted only five brief items in the scrapbook which he devoted to clippings. One of these critiques, not identified by Kennedy, once again compared the author with Irving and admonished the public: "Let us encourage our own literature, now we have it." Another reviewer, writing in a Maryland newspaper, found it "full of instruction" and admired "the spirit of toleration." The strictures on the book were comparatively trivial. One commentator thought that Kennedy might have drawn the chapter epigraphs from American sources rather than from Scott, Goldsmith, and the English playwrights. Another shuddered at the oaths but complained that there were not enough "surprise" elements in the plot.[12] Only Burton's *Gentleman's Magazine* among the better known literary periodicals took space to discuss it—in an article which lumped *Rob* in with several other new works.

The author who had reveled in the public attention which his first two books had brought him was baffled by this general apathy, though in a letter to a friend he softened the blow for himself:

> I was aware it was not likely to be so popular as 'Horse Shoe Robinson.' The tale is somewhat antiquated in date, required a somewhat obsolete phraseology and a description of ancient manners—ancient, I mean, in our calendar. Still, I like it, better than 'Horse Shoe'—perhaps first for the natural reason that it is the youngest born, and secondly, because it required more antiquarian labor, in which, by the way, I take some pride.[13]

It is probably impossible to ascertain precisely why one book caught on in the 1830's and another failed, but certainly the reason was not inherent in the story, which was at least a cut above the average popular romance of the day. One factor was competition from the annually growing list of books pirated from foreign sources on which no royalties had to be paid. Another was the fact—which Cooper and Simms also discovered—that the loud calls for a native literature had now brought a large number of champions into the field, and the achievement of one or two successes was no guarantee that a writer could hold an audience by the mere familiarity of his name. Nearly fifty new American works of fiction were issued in this year 1838 alone; among their authors were rivals of Kennedy like Cooper, Robert Montgomery Bird, Joseph Holt Ingraham, Poe, and Simms.[14]

But whatever the cause of the poor financial showing of *Rob of the Bowl,* the experience made Kennedy less eager to jeopardize his other interests by further time-consuming forays into fiction. On the final page of *Rob* he had held out the promise of a sequel: "We part, I would even indulge the hope, but for a short period; after which we may find motive to look again into the little city and renew our acquaintance." But the motive was not to be found again, and Kennedy's brief but significant career as a writer of native historical fiction came to an abrupt conclusion.

CHAPTER 5

Quodlibet: Equality Hall

I *The Leveling Trend*

IN LATE 1838 KENNEDY had been riding high on the crest of his literary and political careers. But the reception of *Rob of the Bowl* was an unexpected disappointment, and during the next year he was defeated in his effort to keep his seat in the House of Representatives. These setbacks gave him both stimulus and opportunity to re-examine at leisure the state of modern American society and the role which he and his party had been playing in the nation's continuing expansion.

Kennedy had by no means given up the idea of further literary composition. Now, however, he felt too involved in contemporary issues to broadcast his views through the more oblique mode of historical fiction. His journals of December, 1839, show that he was yearning to write a topical book about the political scene; but finding a format for such a project proved something of a struggle. At first he considered building his critique around the figure of a landholder who would observe and comment on the occupations and opinions of the people of his neighborhood—perhaps in the vein of somewhat similar sections in *Swallow Barn*. Again, he thought of jettisoning a narrative framework altogether and simply composing a set of formal disquisitions under the portentous heading of "Estimate of the Character, Principles and Manners of the United States." And, in a third tentative plan, he pondered discussing his subjects "in a series of informal, irregular essays, presenting the topics without any indicated method, and adopting the grave style, the satircial, the ludicrous, the dramatic or the narrative as the purpose of the moment might prompt." He then added: "Upon a review of these suggestions I incline to the latter and shall forthwith set about the undertaking."[1] He was as good as his word, for a further entry of the same month notes: "Sat down to my book and wrote a portion of the 1st Chapter, 'The People' —It will not be the first in order."

For some time he continued to confide to his notebooks notions about social order in the United States and the origins and organization of its political parties. These draft essays may make dull reading today, but they are useful in putting into perspective many of the themes which he had already developed in his three works of fiction. He was more than ever preoccupied with the clash between tradition and progress, between an established land-owning class and the mob of city dwellers, between the efforts to maintain a native aristocracy and the leveling tendencies which had culminated in Jacksonian democracy. Indeed, Jacksonianism became identified as the principal villain as Kennedy sought to understand contemporary unrest—and his own defeat at the polls. The United States, so he observed, had now been split into three classes. The best citizens were, he believed, unfortunately too tied up with their own affairs and too distrustful of the machinery of politics to wield power as they might. Meanwhile, the second class—the idle and ignorant—and the third—political job-holders—were in command and were subverting the original aims of the republic. A probable cure, he thought, would be to overturn the spoils system itself and take away from the President the power to confer office as a reward for party hacks. But, whatever the panacea, Kennedy longed for immediate action.[2]

As Kennedy mulled over his criticism of the contemporary scene, he hit upon a way to present his message in a more palatable form. He would create and describe a mythical borough that would represent America under Jacksonian rule, and he would employ the ironic mode for exposing its dangerous follies. And so, during this presidential election year of 1840, when his Whigs were booming William Henry Harrison and John Tyler as their ticket against the Democrats' Martin Van

Buren, he offered as ammunition the book which he called *Quodlibet*. By his own account its composition was swift:

> [I]n the months of June, July and August, [1840], working in the intervals of severer exercise, I wrote Quodlibet, which I placed in the hands of Lea & Blanchard on the 20th of August, with directions to publish it anonymously. They did so. The book appeared in the first week of September. It was remarkably well received by those who read it, but the excitement of the Canvass [the presidential race] was too great to allow it to find an extensive circulation. Since the Canvass has closed, Quodlibet is finding its way into a more extensive acquaintance. The press attributes it to various persons.

In form *Quodlibet* purports to be the "authentic account of the origin and growth of the borough" of Quodlibet as recorded by one Solomon Secondthoughts, a schoolmaster; the time span stretches from the Jackson administration to the Harrison-Van Buren campaign. In the view of the narrator, the chief event in the history of the town had been the culminating act in President Jackson's war on the United States Bank: the moment when, in the fall of 1833, he had ordered Federal deposits removed from that institution and placed in what came to be known as "pet banks." From this date, and under the continued benign reign of the Democrats, Quodlibet had prospered; but Kennedy's technique is, of course, to convince the reader that the actual truth is always the opposite of the proud boasts of Secondthoughts.

The story line develops through a series of incidents: the establishment of the Patriotic Copperplate Bank, the development of the aristocratic Middleton Flam into a New Light Democrat, political rallies, party splits, the collapse of the bank, and other "historical" events. Kennedy's satirical thrusts are sometimes heavy-handed, sometimes delightfully oblique. The attack on leveling and the rule of the ignorant majority is rather flatly done, as when the Honorable Middleton Flam changes the name of his classical-style country seat from Quality Hall to Equality Hall and his neighborhood from Poplar Flats to Popular Flats. But Kennedy has a subtle touch in the name of his narrator, Secondthoughts, which alludes to the remark of

Van Buren that "the sober, second thought of the people is never wrong." And, when the reader recalls Shelley's poem, he can see another neat hit in the fact that the Patriotic Cooperplate Bank is an "exact miniature copy of the Tomb of Osymandias."[3] Moreover, the style of Secondthoughts—by turns pedantic, mock Classical, painfully humorous, and wittily witless—is cleverly contrived; it matches some of the best passages of *Swallow Barn.* Here, for example, is Secondthoughts' introduction of himself and his subject:

> By the aid of my early patron the judge, whose memory will long be embalmed in the unction of my gratitude, I became, after Master Middleton was passed from under my care, the head of our district school, which at first was established in that lowly log building under the big chestnut upon the Rumblebottom, about fifty rods south of Christy M'Curdy's mill; which tenement is yet to be seen, although in a melancholy state of desolation, the roof thereof having been blown away in the famous hurricane of August 1836, just two years and ten months after the Removal of the Deposites. This unfortunate event—I mean the blowing off of the roof—it was the mercy of Providence to delay for the term of one year and a fraction of a month after I had removed into the new academy which my former pupil, and now, in lineal succession to his lamented parent the Judge, my second patron, the Hon. Middleton Flam, had procured to be erected for my better accomodation in the Borough of Quodlibet. Had my removal been delayed, or the hurricane have risen thirteen months sooner than it did who shall tell what mourning it might not have spread through our country side;—who shall venture to say that Quodlibet might not have been to-day without a chronicler? (xix)

Kennedy can also deftly deflate the pompous and hypocritical oratory of the smooth politician, as in this maundering of Agamemnon Flag:

> "I see before me a vast concourse of free citizens—the solid, substantial, durable, permanent, everlasting pillars of free government. The honest, upright, pure, hardhanded, horny-fisted, Democratic yeomanry of the country are here—not the flesh and blood of the country, for that is the pampered aristocracy—but the bone and sinew surround me. It rejoices my eyes to behold these honest, sturdy, independent, intelligent, invincible tillers of the

> soil—these brawny, unconquerable, liberty-loving working-men—I say sir, I delight to look upon them; my feeble vision, sir——"
> "Put on your specs, Ag!" shouted Ben Inky and Flan Sucker. . . . (123)

But in spite of its wit and occasional sharp strokes, *Quodlibet* is today a dead book. Parrington, it is true, called it "the most vivacious criticism of Jacksonianism in our political library" and concluded that it was "one of our few distinguished political satires."[4] Yet the fact remains that the satire is chiefly directed at a specific contemporary situation, and only the special student of this period can grasp all the secondary meanings. Kennedy fancied that he was writing in the tradition of the Neo-Classical satirists (and perhaps that, too, of Irving in *Knickerbocker's History of New York*), but his subject is too parochial to allow any more universal application. He himself, not unnaturally, thought highly of his "annals." To his uncle he boasted: "I shall take an opportunity to send you a new work which I know will greatly delight you—Quodlibet. You will find it a veritable history of the [United States Bank] war, and afford you a good laugh. When you have read it, send it to my mother for her perusal. She is politician enough to relish the battering of the enemy."[5] Some of the reviewers also enjoyed the battering, but critical opinion of the book was predictably split along partisan lines. Commercially it was not a success; Lea & Blanchard had printed 1,500 copies on a fifty-fifty profit-sharing basis, but Kennedy gleaned only about $100 from the sales.

Quodlibet was not reissued until 1860, when Lippincott included it in a new edition of Kennedy's works. Kennedy made a few changes in the text, including the addition of a postscript describing the election of Harrison; but his preface for the reprint acknowledged that, after a lapse of only twenty years, his book was already chiefly of antiquarian interest to new readers. Yet, he felt, it might also serve to demonstrate to a younger generation the fact that the heated political quarrels in which men engaged passed quickly away:

> May it not serve a good turn toward arresting this torrent of innovation, to present to the leisure meditation of those who are embarking upon its stream, a few memorials of a bygone

> day, quite as distinguished as the present for the intensity of its political ardors and the absurdity of its excesses, but, fortunately, more harmless and amiable in its temper? Is it not worth while to attempt, by these playful sketches of the past, to lure the angry combatants into a smile, and, by showing them the grotesque retribution which history inflicts upon distempered parties after a few decades of oblivion, to beguile them into some consideration of the predicament in which they may leave their own renown?

Moreover, Kennedy insisted upon the permanent validity of his picture of American politics. "History is constantly reproducing itself," he contended. "Events have different dates, and run in different names; but motives, human action and passion, are the same, and bring to light the same categories of thought and opinion. That which has been, is, and will be again, through an infinite series of repetitions."[6] This is good Neo-Classic doctrine, but it is irrelevant to the merits and defects of *Quodlibet*. Nothing but laborious footnoting could really restore full meaning to the text, and few readers would find the result worth such a venture.

II *Wirt Remembered*

Kennedy's next literary project would be a biography of William Wirt, the brilliant Baltimore lawyer and author to whom he had dedicated *Swallow Barn*. But he was absorbed during the early 1840's in the myriad details of his other occupations, and the book had to await its turn. His services to his party had not gone unrecognized. Following the victory of Harrison and Tyler, he was offered the post of under secretary by Harrison's chosen Secretary of State, Daniel Webster; but Kennedy refused the honor on the grounds that he hoped to regain his seat in the national House. The Whigs were thrown into turmoil when Harrison died just a month after his inauguration, but Kennedy did manage again to win election as a representative in May, 1841. During this and a succeeding term he found himself in the center of the party rebellion against the anti-bank policies of John Tyler, who had succeeded to the presidency. Tyler, as unbending a Virginian as the proprietor of Swallow Barn, was no lightweight opponent; and Kennedy was increasingly appalled that a man who had worn the party label could be so treacherous —and so powerful.[7]

Two political documents were the fruit of these years: the "Whig Manifesto" (1841) and *The Defense of the Whigs* (1844). Neither is properly an item in Kennedy's literary career; but, like *Quodlibet,* they are useful statements of the doctrines upon which his other books were grounded. The first, the "Manifesto," which he composed with some aid from Henry Clay, tried to expel Tyler from the party for his disregard of fundamental Whig doctrines. Tyler only sneered that Kennedy ought to stick to writing romances. The second document, the *Defense,* was a more ambitious attempt to reinterpret the history of the chief political parties. With more zeal than absolute accuracy, Kennedy identified two antithetical lines of power as continuous in America since pre-Revolutionary days. The first was the "Court" party or Tories, namely the modern-day Democrats; the second was the "Country" party or Whigs. The former, in his view, consistently favored a strong executive branch; the latter, a strong national legislature.

As always in his political writings, Kennedy sought to counter attacks upon the Whigs as the champion of the moneyed class; he was particularly sensitive here since he was being ridiculed in the opposition press as "aristocratical." But his carefully reasoned *Defense,* which also continued his pommeling of Tyler, made little stir in the country at large; and he gained nothing tangible for his trouble. However, the whole feud with Tyler, as Charles H. Bohner has pointed out,[8] effectively put an end to any sentimental attachment for Virginia which might have lingered in Kennedy's memory. The hardheadedness at which he had once smiled in Frank Meriwether could no longer appear very amusing.

During his service in Congress Kennedy also busied himself with the support of such projects as Samuel F. B. Morse's telegraph and an international copyright agreement, but he was gradually growing weary of Washington life and politics. His own economic conservatism, his desire to keep power in the hands of the propertied, his distrust of popular democracy—all these brought him into daily conflict with the opposition forces; he was not, therefore, eager to seek-election in 1845. His health too had suffered (he had long been annoyed by a severe eczema of the face); and he wanted, so he said, free time to return once more to his literary interests. Escaping political wrangles for a Northern trip in the summer of 1845, he and his family went to call on James Fenimore Cooper at his fanciful house, Otsego Hall; Cooper insisted on escorting the party to a scene described in *The Pioneers*, and the band of romantic adventurers were drenched in a cloudburst on a mountain-top.

Kennedy came back from this memorable vacation to learn that he was once more the choice of the local Whigs for the congressional seat; but, when the Democrats swept into office in the fall voting, he was again out of power. Though he had wanted leisure, it was hard to quit. In 1846-47 he accepted service in the Maryland legislature, the scene of his earliest political triumphs; and this time he was made Speaker of the House of Delegates. But his influence as a politician was rapidly waning; and, when he was again nominated for Congress in 1847, he suffered an embarrassing defeat. He now firmly resolved never to run again. He had, after all, several occupations to which he could turn. There was, for one thing, the long-postponed biography of Wirt.

The task had originally promised to be a congenial one. Kennedy had found in Wirt an early friend and patron, and he had admired the elder man's *Letters of the British Spy* (1803) and *Sketches of the Life and Character of Patrick Henry* (1817). As a renowned member of the local bar and as Attorney General under Presidents Monroe and Adams, Wirt had been a figure of some importance during the early days of the republic; Kennedy no doubt believed that he could make the biography not only a tribute to Wirt himself but also a respectable addition to the small shelf of his own writings. Wirt's widow originally had asked John Quincy Adams to edit his papers and to prepare a life, but old age had forced Adams to surrender the project. In December, 1843, after seeking elsewhere for a successor, Mrs. Wirt turned to Kennedy. In a journal entry for that month noting Adams' withdrawal, he commented: "The family have since committed it to me, and I have accepted."[9] It was not until March 1, 1846, however that he rather guiltily recorded, "this day began *to write* the Biography." By July of the same year he was already disillusioned: "Wirt's life comes on slowly. It is a great drag. I wish some body else had it." Kennedy's defeat for Congress in late 1847 finally allowed him the time he required to return to it in earnest, but other subjects kept springing into his mind. On his fifty-second birthday—October 25, 1847—he jotted down these random ideas:

> I am at work upon my Life of Wirt—and somewhat inclined to be busy with other literary speculations. I want to write a series of essays, somewhat after the manner of Southey's 'Doctor,'—with all sorts of experiences—I would call it Ethos—Custom—and make its drift to point out the tyrannies of custom over the mind and conduct of men.
>
> I have another fancy—to write a satire and call it Young America. It should represent the career of an impudent, ignorant, flippant pretender to knowledge[,] patriotism and virtue—a thorough scamp, in whose history I would embody all the horrible things of Locofocoism.
>
> —Besides these I hope to write a comedy. I wish to try my hand on a good comedy—what kind I have not yet settled, but I will digest a plan.
>
> —I think I can make up a volume out of my own writings which have been published heretofore in periodicals and newspapers—something like a set of essays—taken from lectures and other dissertations I have written.
>
> A volume too I could make of statistics and political discussion out of my speeches, reports and other public matter which has heretofore been published.
>
> Another crotchet I have—to republish Swallow Barn, Horse Shoe, Rob of the Bowl and Quodlibet, with some emendations.[10]

But the biography of Wirt still demanded to be finished first. It was not meticulousness alone—or even a growing boredom with his subject—that made Kennedy so dilatory. He had naturally relied on finding nearly all he needed among Wirt's many letters and papers, but he had discovered that he would be required to do much outside research. Still active in his own law practice and called upon more and more by his father-in-law to deal with the affairs of Gray's mills, Kennedy had to sandwich in periods for the gathering of his data; the spring of 1849 had rolled around before he completed his first draft. Now at last he could move more swiftly. Lea & Blanchard contracted to publish the new work, and their two-volume edition reached the public in late September, 1849.

Despite all the care which Kennedy lavished upon it, *The Life of William Wirt* is for the modern reader a dreary production. Since it was intended to be commemorative, the reader would expect to find Wirt's virtues magnified and his faults minimized—yet he would nonetheless anticipate some life in a *Life*. Unfortunately it has little; it is padded out with Wirt's documents (which were freely edited and altered); it is slanted according to Kennedy's own political views; it is "official" in all the bad senses of that word. Yet it received several excellent reviews and had a substantial sale; reprinted within a month, it was destined to go through six editions. As both reviews and sales confirmed, writing a biography was still more "respectable" than turning out a popular romance; and Kennedy's contemporary reputation accordingly rose. But he was also a businessman who believed in fair compensation for his labor, and the accounting which he set down in his journal of the proceeds from the first edition has a sour tone:

Total proceeds of a popular work which sells an edition of 1,000 in one month, after deducting 71 copies given away, and the remaining 929 selling at 4.50	$4180.50
Which sum is distributed as follows:	
To the author, after two years hard work	568.50
To the mechanics who got up the book with 5 months hard work	1650.00
To the booksellers for one month's very light work	1962.00
	$4180.50

"It is," he could only conclude, "an edifying exhibition of the profits of bookmaking."[11]

III *Revival*

The idea of such poor return after so much mental and physical labor apparently continued to gall Kennedy, for sixteen months later he attempted a complete casting up of all his literary earnings to that date. The tabulation proved just as "edifying":

Swallow Barn, published in 1832:		
One edition—2,000 copies—gave me altogether		$782.69
Horse Shoe, 1835 and '36. Two editions:		
1st. 3,000 copies	$1,200	
2d. 3,000 ———	500	
		1700.00
Rob of the Bowl, 1838, 4,000 copies		1850.00
Quodlibet, 1840, 1,500 copies		100.00
Defense of the Whigs, 1844, 4,000 copies published by Harper & Brothers		nothing
Life of Wirt, 1st edition, 1849:		
1,000 copies published on division [of] profits. My share	$568.50	
One half I gave to Mrs. Wirt	284.25	
Net amt. to me		284.25
Ditto, 2d edition, 1850:		
3,000 copies at 25 cents	$750	
Ditto, 2d edition, 1851:		
750 copies at 30 cents	225	
		975.00
Total receipts to this date		$5691.94[12]

This was a sorry showing indeed for more than twenty years of active authorship, but Kennedy was by no means ready to let his books slip into total obscurity merely because they did not pay well. In 1845 he had tried to interest Lea & Blanchard in bringing out reprints, but his long-time publishers were apathetic. His "crotchet" to reissue revised editions, however, made him go on seeking; and in the early 1850's the opportunity finally presented itself. George P. Putnam of New York had recently been printing collections of the works of Irving and Cooper; on April 9, 1851, he and Kennedy signed an agreement for a new edition of *Swallow Barn,* to be illustrated by David Strother, an artist-writer friend who was to become well known under the pseudonym "Porte Crayon." Putnam promised a royalty rate of 12½ per cent, the same reward as that given to Irving and Cooper.

With the appearance of the revised *Swallow Barn* in September, 1851, Kennedy luxuriated in cheering sales and friendly, retrospective reviews. Mindful of the stir caused by the Compromise of 1850, he had carefully checked over the passages concerning slavery in the hope that his book might contribute to the calming of aroused tempers. Basically, his position remained the same as it had been in 1832: he considered slavery an evil from a moral standpoint, but the Abolition Movement was still worse because, if successful, it would bring sudden economic ruin to the entire South. Southern reviewers were on the whole delighted by his moderate position; one anonymous commentator, whose notice Kennedy pasted in his scrapbook, adopted a typically self-righteous tone:

> It would be well for our Northern friends to take some pains to get information on this subject, and to understand it rightly. Nothing is more absurd than the summary and wholesale conclusions to which fanaticism jumps, with its sweeping dogmas of abstract rights and the rights of men, when it undertakes to judge of a relation which is modified and necessitated by a thousand considerations and circumstances, and in which the party most benefitted is the one which they consider to be aggrieved, and to be entitled to all their sympathies. The class that would suffer most from a dissolution of the relation between master and slave in the southern states is the servile class, who could not maintain themselves at all if detached from the support of the stronger class.[13]

Simms also rejoiced in the reissue, though he realized that he and Kennedy were poles apart politically; and he saw to it that *Swallow Barn* received a long review in the influential *Southern Quarterly Review,* which he was then editing.[14] Kennedy's brother, Philip Pendleton, however, objected that the passages on slavery were intrusive and not relevant to the dramatic action of the book. Kennedy's response is revealingly irritable:

> What do you mean by the modern dissertation on slavery in Swallow Barn? What you refer to is what was published in the first edition with some modifications which I thought would improve it in the revision. The didactic character is not altered, nor the opinion on any material point. I agree that this passage is a departure from the dramatic character, but it struck me in writing that chapter that it furnished a good occasion for some grave opinions on slavery which might be useful North and South. And in confirmation of this these passages have been extracted in several papers and commented on with approbation. —One is obliged to be useful, now and then, you know, even at the risk of waking up a dreamer from a pleasant sleep.[15]

Simms, in a personal letter in which he hailed the reappearance of *Swallow Barn,* had urged Kennedy now to turn to new subjects and to produce further historical romances: "Braddock's career is properly left to you. The material besides, in the same region, is both abundant & rich. Boone, Rogers, Clarke, & others, afford ample room & verge enough to the writer of prose fiction; & by making yourself familiar with the scene, (which is an important matter) you have all that is necessary to your hands."[16]

But Kennedy was primarily interested in getting additional mileage out of his old vehicles; and, with the success of the revised *Swallow Barn,* he found Putnam quite ready to proceed immediately with a reissue of *Horse-Shoe Robinson.* The well-known illustrator F. O. C. Darley, who also did drawings for the collected editions of Simms and Cooper, was assigned to the book; and, with a few relatively unimportant alterations, it was ready in late April, 1852. Simms, ever mindful of his own rigorous efforts to have South Carolina recognized as a leader in the Revolutionary War, was not so well pleased with *Horse-Shoe.* "You will see," he wrote Kennedy in July, 1852, informing him of his forthcoming notice in the *Southern Quarterly Review,* "that I join issue with you upon certain points of your Historical Summary, and suggest some shortcomings in the details of the story, such as I could have wished that you had revised for the New Ed."[17] *Horse-Shoe,* however, still found a number of ready readers; and in 1854 Putnam was stimulated to bring out the third of the early books, *Rob of the Bowl.*

Kennedy had now achieved his ambition to have his fiction put before a new audience; but, whether or not he realized the fact, his era in American literature was rapidly drawing to a close. In this decade of the 1850's the earlier generation of fiction writers—Irving, Cooper, Simms—received their proper tribute in the form of handsome collected editions; but it was Hawthorne and Melville who were producing work which fully realized the potentialities of the romance genre. Kennedy could not have followed the ways opened up by these subtler artists. He developed little as a writer during the 1830's, when he first came to prominence, and—despite his pride in achievement—he never gave himself fully to the literary craft. He had done what he could do in sustained bursts of work in intervals between his many other duties. And that, for him, was enough.

CHAPTER *6*

'Calm Repose and Social Culture'

I *The Rewards of Party*

ELATED AS HE WAS by the reissues of his three stories, Kennedy must still have recognized that in an oblique way he was confessing that he could not add new work to this small shelf. The incredible productivity of his acquaintance Simms he had no hope of emulating; in 1846, after Simms had dedicated *Count Julian* to him, Kennedy had modestly replied:

> I hope you will acquit me of any very earnest opinion that my *labors* (holiday sports rather) in our common field have entitled me to the rank which your dedication would seem to infer. I am no better than a laggard in the glorious path where you have become a leader, yet still have enough of the *esprit du corps* about me to take pleasure in the contemplation of your distinguished career. You may always count upon me as one to vindicate your claim to the high reputation you have earned in the literature of our country, and, if nothing more, you will, at least, find me a good bottle-holder whenever you have occasion to enter the ring.[1]

And, a few years later, he was still telling Simms, who had been nagging at him to contribute to the *Southern Quarterly Review*:

> I greet all your letters with a most earnest welcome, and always with a little envy at the proof they give me of your industry. You work, whilst I only talk of it. I have a hundred projects only—to set off against your hundred performances. Every mail almost—often enough to say *every*—brings me something of yours done. My time is absorbed, *wasted,* with the little villainous

> shuffles of the business of the day—letters—an occasional railroad report—an *infernal* lecture, now and then, and dribblets of occupation which leave me no time to write *what I have in hand.* I spend five or six hours a day in my library,—I have hardly an hour a day to read print. . . . I am the busiest man in Baltimore. . . .[2]

During the nineteen years of life remaining to him, Kennedy was often to sound this plaintive note. He simply could not avoid fragmenting his time. Though he had given up the idea of actively seeking elective office, he was unable to keep himself detached from the fortunes of the Whigs. In the early 1850's, while tempers were inflamed by the slavery issue and the specter of secession, he was mentioned for several state and national posts; but no appointments materialized. Yet even out of power he pleaded the cause of union; in an article in the Washington *National Intelligencer* for March 2, 1850, he castigated current talk of disruption as "the fancy of phrenzied minds heated to an unwholesome temperature by too much pondering over imaginary griefs." The country at large had prospered too greatly—with its railroads, factories, steamers, expanding borders—to permit dissidents to cut the ties which bound all the states. The most powerful disruptive forces he saw as adamant Northern Abolitionism on the one side and Southern fire-eating on the other, but he hoped that the Whigs could appeal to reasonable men in both sections. At considerable cost to himself, since Baltimore had many Southern sympathizers, Kennedy maintained his strong Union position through the terrible years which followed. And to the end he remained a spokesman to whom his colleagues listened.

In 1852 he crowned his political career by accepting from his old friend President Fillmore an interim appointment to the post of Secretary of the Navy. The cabinet job was no sinecure, but his tenure was a brief eight months. He was a strong supporter of the expedition of Commodore Matthew C. Perry, which opened up Japan, and the search by Dr. Elisha Kane for the British explorer Sir John Franklin; he was also a prime mover in the organization of surveying voyages to Africa, South America, and the northern Pacific. His report on naval affairs for 1852 won him many plaudits, including election to the American Philosophical Society.[3]

But the Whig party, rent by internal conflicts over national policy on such matters as slavery, was dying; and, with the election of the Democrat Franklin Pierce to the presidency in 1852, Kennedy's days on the political stage were over. Defeat, however, was tempered by the arrival in Washington of two literary lions, Irving and William Makepeace Thackeray, the latter then on a lecture tour of the nation. With both his early idol and the current sensation as his personal guests, he could feel that recognition was being paid not only to his official rank but also to his own status as an author.

In the years following his political apotheosis, Kennedy settled down into a routine of business and public service which lasted until his death in 1870. This period is properly the province of the biographer and not the student of literature, but its outlines are worth recording in order to show why Kennedy only rarely again concerned himself with creative writing. He was financially well off; with the prosperity of the Gray cotton mills he could afford the luxuries of a new house, a well-stocked library, and pleasant summer holidays. In local affairs he kept his post as provost of the University of Maryland; and he was one of those chosen to organize the Peabody Institute, the gift to the city of the financier George Peabody, with whom Kennedy had served during the War of 1812. The Institute, which was planned to include a library, an art gallery, and a conservatory of music, Kennedy served well as president for a decade; and the bequest to it of his personal papers is evidence of his hopes for its future role in Baltimore's cultural life. Other organizations also called upon him; when three railroads were merged into the Northern Central Railroad Company, he accepted the presidency with pleasure at this further evidence of local progress.

But, despite all these concerns, Kennedy was now finding more time for recreation and travel. In 1854 he and former President Fillmore made a tour of the lower South which was a personal triumph for both men. Two years later Kennedy's father-in-law died after a long and trying illness, and he took his wife and sister-in-law on an excursion to Europe. They were away only a few months since Kennedy wished to return to see how Fillmore would fare in the national election in the autumn. But, when his friend was swamped in a contest which saw the rise of the Republican party as a major power, he at last knew that the days of the Whigs had ended; he and his wife now returned to Europe for a stay which lasted fifteen months. The sojourn had come too late to have any effect upon his writing. Irving and Cooper had sought the European perspective while still engaged in their active careers, and Hawthorne had at this very time been observing "our old home" while acting as consul in Liverpool.

Like his fellow authors, Kennedy kept voluminous notebook records of his journeys; but, unlike Hawthorne, who came to call on him in Rome, he did not contemplate using his experiences abroad as material for new romances. Indeed, as he grew older, he began to regret that his reputation as a writer had been won largely by his tales. "What little position I have in the literary world is connected only with my few works of fiction," he wrote to George Putnam, his recent publisher. "It has sometimes occurred to me that I do myself injustice in assuming a stand exclusively upon that ground."[4] He wanted, therefore, to reissue *Quodlibet* and his *Life of Wirt*. Further, he planned to publish a volume of essays on serious topics, including a discussion of the relations between Great Britain and the United States.[5] *Quodlibet* and *Wirt* were finally brought out by Lippincott in 1860; the three earlier books were also reprinted from the plates stereotyped by Putnam in the early 1850's.

Of the few new productions of Kennedy's later years, only one deserves brief mention here. This is the narrative, based upon his researches in the state archives, which he called "A Legend of Maryland." In final form it appeared in the July and August, 1860, issues of the *Atlantic Monthly;* an earlier version he had read before the Maryland Institute and then published in a local newspaper and in the *Southern Literary Messenger.*[6] The "Legend" has many links with *Rob of the Bowl;* it traces incidents in the life of Colonel George Talbot (a minor figure in that romance), and it discusses some of the materials which Kennedy had previously employed. Kennedy's purpose here was to seek the historical facts behind popular legends connected with Talbot's name, though he skillfully maintained the suspense of a good mystery story. What is most interesting today, however, is the introductory material in which he made explicit his theory that it is the creative writer alone who can take the dry bones of history and reconstruct some semblance to living creatures; it is he who visualizes and then dramatizes actions which documents merely record:

> [T]hat which makes history the richest of philosophies and the most genial pursuit of humanity is the spirit that is breathed into it by the thoughts and feelings of former generations, interpreted in actions and incidents that disclose the passions, motives, and ambition of men, and open to us a view of the actual life of our forefathers. When we can contemplate the people of a past age employed in their own occupations, observe their habits and manners, comprehend their policy and their methods of pursuing it, our imagination is quick to clothe them with the flesh and blood of human brotherhood and to bring them into full sympathy with our individual nature. History then becomes a world of living figures,—a theatre that presents to us a majestic drama, varied by alternate scenes of the grandest achievements and the most touching episodes of human existence.[7]

It is significant that Kennedy had returned in imagination to seventeenth-century Maryland in this last year before the outbreak of the Civil War; for the earlier period, too, had once been one of internal conflicts. And now he would himself live through four years of disruption, years when his staunch loyalty to the Union brought him much personal recrimination. In late December, 1860, when South Carolina had already seceded, he wrote a pamphlet entitled *The Border States: Their Power and Duty in the Present Disordered Condition of the Country.* Its plea was that the states in the zone between North and deep South should immediately try to effect a compromise. But the war erupted within months, and he watched his relatives and friends at home and in Virginia march off to fight either as Union or Confederate soldiers. In Baltimore, where Southern sentiment remained strong, he was snubbed on the street by old friends; but he would not swerve from his old unionist faith

—a fact noted by Harvard College in 1863 when it conferred upon him the degree of Doctor of Laws.

During 1863 and 1864 Kennedy contributed to the *National Intelligencer* a series of essays outlining the Northern conservative position; these were collected in 1865 as *Mr. Ambrose's Letters on the Rebellion*—the last of his books to be published during his lifetime. By the close of the war he was in poor health and aging rapidly; in a effort to recuperate, he spent the early months of 1866 in Cuba, stopping in Charleston on the homeward journey for a brief reunion with the equally broken Simms. Back in Baltimore, he failed to improve; and in one final effort to restore his health, he soon set out on a third tour of Europe. In the more than two years abroad he managed to travel rather extensively, but the end was now not far away. His last months were spent in a vain attempt to alleviate the crippling rheumatism and the abdominal pains from which he had suffered since the war era. Finally, on August 18, 1870, death came to Kennedy in Newport, Rhode Island, where he had gone for a summer visit. He had lived from the post-Revolutionary period to the threshold of the Gilded Age. In the next few decades the tremendous industrial and physical expansion of which he had so long dreamed became a reality. But the corruption and the political radicalism of the new age could only have appalled him.

Kennedy's death attracted due attention. As befitted a man who had contributed so significantly to the business and political affairs of the nation, most of the tributes emphasized the public figure rather than the writer. A typical obituary comment was that of the Baltimore *American*:

> Our distinguished fellow-citizen, John Pendleton Kennedy, has gone to his rest. In these days of intense and one-sided development is there not a lesson for us in his useful life? When the material progress of the age overshadows the growth of individual character, is it not well to pause and ask ourselves what is the secret of this life in which personal influence seems to make the man so much greater than his works? It is that he was not an extremist, that he gave scope to the development of his character. A man of wealth, he did not labor to acquire untold riches; a man of leisure, he was not an idler, but dedicated

his energies to politics and literature. His worthy ambitions and noble aims were not debased to the passions of power and success. His was not a surface life, but was softened by the Rembrandt back-ground of calm repose and social culture. . . . He might have written better novels if all his energies had been given to novel writing; he might have held high offices if he had taxed his strength in the race for power; he might have become a merchant prince if he had consecrated his life and wealth to the mammon of unrighteousness; but in each instance he would have sacrificed *himself*. . . .[8]

James Russell Lowell, a personal friend, recalled that "His talk had just that pleasant suspicion of scholarship in it that befits the drawing-room, and never degenerated to the coarser flavor of pedantry." As a creative writer, Kennedy was, in Lowell's estimation, one "who simply knew how to be agreeable. I think Mr. Kennedy's books have this pleasant quality,—a secret not seldom missed by writers more pretentious and of greater power."[9] But this praise is not very acute; and indeed it was difficult to see the real merits of Kennedy's old-fashioned romances in the early 1870's when the careers of the foremost authors of the Realistic period—William Dean Howells, Mark Twain, and Henry James—had already begun. But now, nearly a century after Kennedy's death, it is possible to estimate more objectively his genuine contributions to the rise of American fiction.

II *Kennedy in Perspective*

As I have observed throughout this study, Kennedy was only secondarily a professional man of letters. He was under no financial pressure to publish; and he shared the notion, common among Southern gentlemen, that the creation of imaginative literature should be subordinate to other occupations. But he was, nevertheless, truly concerned that America develop an indigenous culture worthy to be ranked with its material gains. He was glad to encourage fellow authors—notably Poe and his own Virginia cousin Philip Pendleton Cooke—and he delighted in his personal associations with Irving, Cooper, Simms, Dickens, Thackeray, and other literary lights of the day.

What most troubled him was that native writing so far had

been primarily sectional. Could a national viewpoint ever be evolved out of such diverse backgrounds? His own residence in the border state of Maryland made him acutely aware of the status of literature in both North and South, and he was dissatisfied with the practice of both regions. New Englanders, he felt, were snobbish; moreover, they too often tended toward abstract philosophizing and involvement in extreme doctrines like Abolitionism. They needed foreign and home-grown competition, and he looked to the South to produce a stimulating challenge. This view he made explicit in a letter addressed to a society at the University of Georgia, which had conferred honorary membership upon him:

> We who live on this nether side of Mason & Dixon's line, have a task to perform which we must not neglect. It is to make a living and exemplary protest against the monopoly of letters which our northern friends are in the habit of claiming for themselves. I say *friends,* because, although I disallow their claims . . . yet I pardon and even admire the emulation which stirs them to the making of this claim. Let us try conclusions with them in that gallant spirit which moved Robin Hood to have a bout with every man of his company, before he would admit him to fellowship, and to like him all the better when he showed manhood enough to beat his captain.[10]

Simms, he felt, should have been the leader in this enterprise since he was not only a prolific producer but also an influential editor. But Simms, like other natives of the deep South, was committed to what Kennedy deplored as "ultraism": blind sectionalism and time-consuming dedication to the defense of local institutions. Kennedy was enough of a Southerner to take pride in the history and legends of the region, but he was also enough of a nationalist to dread the South's growing isolationism.

His ideal of an American literature, then, was yet to be attained. He wanted the writers of all areas to place nationalism above sectionalism, moderation above extremism, enlightenment above mere entertainment. He looked for the sort of novel which could make all his fellow citizens aware of their gloriously diverse inheritance from the past and at the same time promote unity and a progressive spirit. Such a book would have the

Neo-Classical virtues of wit, clarity of style, and concern for form; it would focus its attention on those societies which Americans had made and could yet make for themselves. Kennedy intended his own three works of fiction as a contribution to this literary program. Today they remain a small but sufficient bequest; they are a still valuable record of one stage in that search for self-knowledge, for national identification, which has always engaged our most significant writers.

My discussions have emphasized this theme—Kennedy's confrontation of the dichotomies in American society—because it appears to me that he has most often been praised for other—and wrong—reasons. Thus, most commentators are content to applaud him as a "stylist" and speak vaguely of his grace or his charm or his "fine technique."[11] But Kennedy's style, while it may be a cut above that of Cooper or of Simms, is not remarkable in itself. He early found the tone he wanted in the Neo-Classical essayists, and his work from *Swallow Barn* on manifests no essential change or development. In comparison with greater contemporaries like Thoreau, Hawthorne, or Melville—men who *did* evolve notable personal styles—Kennedy sounds like a voice from a vanished day.

Again, it has been customary for critics to make a claim for the "historical accuracy" and the "realism" of his fiction and find his books of enduring worth because they are based upon genuine records or memories of the American past. However, as I have tried to demonstrate, Kennedy's chief interest in history was what he called its "majestic drama"; he wished to reveal behind an apparently rootless American culture links with the greater human society. Obviously, he was concerned not to misrepresent the facts or be consciously anachronistic. But he was not an objective inquirer into the historical record; he always drew just what he wanted from it in order to make his own imaginative reconstruction.

It has been my contention throughout this study that *Swallow Barn, Horse-Shoe Robinson,* and *Rob of the Bowl* have only negligible value as authentic portraits of the periods which they presume to represent; much more usefully, they can now be seen as the fantasies of an alert, intelligent—and nervous—writer of the 1830's who employed the vehicle of fiction in an attempt to resolve the dilemmas which the national experience had created. For the experiences of his own life had made Kennedy deeply conscious of the fact that—in Henry James's words—being an American was a complex fate. He was an apostle of progress who nonetheless thought it important to uncover the bonds which linked the present with the past. He was a materialistic businessman-politician who sought spiritual values in the creation of national legend. He was an aristocrat by temperament who dedicated himself to the ideals of a republic.

All of his books are fundamentally concerned with one haunting question: who should lead in a democracy? In his fiction he examined the claims of a native nobility: the plantation gentry in *Swallow Barn,* Lindsay and Butler in *Horse-Shoe Robinson,* the "Cavaliers" in *Rob of the Bowl.* All of these characters are reflections of Kennedy's belief that America had once had an ordered society in which the conservative values were pre-eminent. But this stability was grounded on disdain of progress and worship of the status quo; in a later generation the result of such influences too often had been regionalism, anti-nationalism, attempted isolationism. Kennedy could only conclude that change was the true American pattern but he also observed that its course had been disconcertingly violent. In the "ancient" Maryland of *Rob of the Bowl,* he showed the Protestant commoners revolting against the rule of the Catholic Lord Proprietary. In *Horse-Shoe Robinson* he depicted a whole nation throwing off the yoke of the past. In *Swallow Barn* he found Virginians of the post-Revolutionary years living quietly in a pleasant dream, but sectionalism and slavery were threatening to transform dream into nightmare.

These stories appear, then, to set up a series of propositions about American society: Americans must remember and respect the past if they are to discover who they are, but they must not live in it. Americans must have an aristocracy of the uncommon man to lead them, but they must beware of the stagnation and "ultraism" of ingrown power. They must believe in the primacy of property rights as the foundation of a stable society. They must even defend the continuation of slavery if sudden emancipation would destroy the economic security of a large segment of the nation. And yet—and yet. What has America progressed from? What is it progressing toward? The questions multiply and the quandary deepens the more its citizens inquire into their origins and hopes.

Kennedy himself tried to remain hopeful about the course of the American republic; he longed to believe that change necessarily meant improvement. But as he followed the fortunes of the Whig party, which he thought offered the best program for an expanding country, he was at times disillusioned. When he was composing *Quodlibet,* he was confident that Jacksonianism could be checked by the right thinkers among the anti-Democrats. But, like his own political fortunes, Whiggery had its ups and downs and, eventually, unforeseen total defeat. When he came to write the preface to the second edition of *Quodlibet* in 1860, he tried to discern some pattern, some cyclical process, in the history of the nation during the first six decades of the nineteenth century; what he extracted from the record was not especially cheering:

> This century has run out its three periods of twenty years. The first ended in the total absorption of all differences of opinion, bringing a stagnant calm upon the waters of ancient strife. [The Missouri Compromise (1820) during the "Era of Good Feelings."] The second culminated in a revolution that shook a great party out of its seat;—a revolution which these annals were designed to illustrate. [The defeat of the Democrats by the Whigs in 1840.] The third period has wheeled through its course, to work another downfall and another revolution more notable and significant than either that have gone before. [The collapse of the Whigs and the increase of sectional strife.]

So change had brought calamity as well as material progress; the nation seemed determined to defeat its own best interests. Still, Kennedy pleaded, the future could yet be made brighter:

> The fourth [period], let us hope, may find a nation restored to reason;—a great united Republic, tried and purified by the experience of dangers incurred and surmounted, and by an awakened patriotism successfully asserting the predominance of the good sense and virtue of the people over the factious spirit that ministers to personal ambition, and the vanity that

> seeks renown in innovations upon either the principles in which the Union was formed, or the sentiment by which it is to be preserved.[12]

It is ironical that, on the eve of the Civil War which was the outcome of the dangerous "ultraism" which Kennedy had so long observed in American society, his three books of fiction appeared to him to be more the records of good old days than critiques. And, as such, he was happy to allow them to be twice reprinted during the decade of the 1860's.

For all his concern with his country's past and future, Kennedy finally lacked the drive which pushed other minor contemporaries—like Simms—to the production of whole shelves of fiction. His ambitions always outran his capabilities; he permitted his days to be split among too many interests. In a reminiscent review of his career, which he set down in his journal on his fifty-ninth birthday in 1854, he frankly recognized these shortcomings:

> I confess to a love of fame—though denying all eagerness or even solicitude in the quest of it. I might have done better for this, with an industry more correspondent to my appreciation of it—and I rather feel some compunction in the thought that by a more useful life, stimulated by an honorable aspiration after the good I had the faculty to accomplish, I might have done more than I have done. I would have worked more zealously in the literary field and have built better monuments for posterity.[13]

And yet it is doubtful that he would have written more or greater books than he produced in the 1830's, even if he had reapportioned his time. He was a modest man, and modest literary renown was all that he really desired. But, for all that, he had worked better than many of his more prolific rivals—better, perhaps, than he himself ever recognized. The contribution which John Pendleton Kennedy made to the American house of fiction was a small and even humble addition; but it was honestly built—and it has weathered the changes of time and fashion surprisingly well.

Notes and References

Chapter One

1. Photostat of original filed with the John Pendleton Kennedy Papers, Peabody Institute Library, Baltimore, Maryland. For a description of these manuscript holdings, see Selected Bibliography. Hereafter in these notes Kennedy Papers will be abbreviated as KP; the title which follows is that given to the bound volume in which the quotation may be found. All of my quotations from Kennedy's manuscripts represent my own transcriptions, in which I have tried to reproduce accurately just what he wrote.

2. William Gilmore Simms, *Count Julian* (Baltimore and New York, 1845), p. v.

3. Biographical data throughout this study are drawn from three principal sources: the Kennedy Papers; Henry T. Tuckerman, *The Life of John Pendleton Kennedy* (New York, 1871); and Charles H. Bohner, *John Pendleton Kennedy: Gentleman from Baltimore* (Baltimore, 1961). Hereafter these latter two biographies will be cited as Tuckerman and Bohner. I have benefited as well from reading William S. Osborne's *John Pendleton Kennedy: A Study of His Literary Career* (Unpublished doctoral dissertation, Columbia University, 1960).

4. KP, An Unfinished Chapter of Autobiography (1834). This is one of three segments of personal reminiscence which Kennedy set down at various times. Unfortunately, none carries his career much beyond his earlier years.

5. KP, Autobiography, pp. 35-36.

6. *Ibid.*, p. 53.

7. The note, dated 1813, is written on the back of a letter preserved in the KP, Letters from Schoolfellows.

8. For a discussion of these essays, see William S. Osborne, " 'The Swiss Traveller' Essays: Earliest Literary Writings of John Pendleton Kennedy," *American Literature*, XXX (May, 1958), 228-33; also Bohner, pp. 29-30.

9. The *Portico,* I (February, 1816), 145.

10. *Swallow Barn* (New York, 1851), p. 149

11. Bohner, p. 74.

12. *Red Book,* I (October 23, 1819), 4-5.

13. *Ibid.,* pp. 34-36.
14. Quoted in Bohner, p. 44.
15. KP, Letters from Schoolfellows, Cruse to Kennedy, January 9, 1821.
16. For a full discussion of this period, see Bohner, pp. 45-71; Tuckerman, pp. 113-19.
17. These articles are preserved in the KP, Vol. No. 41, labelled "Scraps" by Kennedy.
18. In 1820 Kennedy had been engaged for a short period to Charlotte Pinkney, daughter of a well-known local lawyer.
19. See, for example, Bohner, p. 66; Parrington's comment is to be found in *Main Currents in American Thought* (New York, 1927), II, 48-49.
20. KP, Journal No. 5, December 25, 1843.
21. Kennedy recorded these and other amusements at various places in his journals for the period.
22. For a full account of the beginnings of American fiction, see Alexander Cowie, *The Rise of the American Novel* (New York, 1948).
23. I have discussed Simms's "myth of the South" at length in my *William Gilmore Simms* in Twayne's United States Authors Series (New York, 1962).

Chapter Two

1. The manuscript of *Swallow Barn,* preserved in the Kennedy Papers, includes a sheaf of unbound notes and drafts of passages which were either dropped from the final version or included in different form.
2. This fragment, called "Studies from Nature by a Young Artist: An Inn," and a succeeding one, "Hoppergallop House," have now been printed for the first time by William S. Osborne in the edition of *Swallow Barn* published by Hafner (New York, 1962), pp. xlvi-lv. My own quotations are taken directly from the manuscripts; the second phrase in brackets in the passage just quoted was lined out by Kennedy.
3. KP, Letters of John Pendleton Kennedy, Vol. II, letter to George P. Putnam, May 3, 1851. *Headlong Hall* (1816) is a novel by Thomas Love Peacock.
4. These conclusions are drawn from an outline filed with the *Swallow Barn* manuscript. The final manuscript itself still reveals traces of early changes of plan. Inked-out, erased, and altered chapter and page numbers show that Kennedy did a fair amount of shifting about of the order of the present Chapters VII to XVIII.

5. Quotations relating to the composition of *Swallow Barn* are taken from the KP, Journal No. 1. Kennedy was fascinated by the history and legends connected with Smith. On November 19 he wrote: "I have been studying the particulars of Capt Smith's life in his own history of Va. and the 2nd vol. of Purchas' Pilgrims p. 1370 et seq. as I intend to introduce the history of this Preux Chevalier into my work." On December 10 he noted that he had recently been occupied in compiling the memoir of Smith from the sources named: "I like it very well, and think it will suit the story of Swallow Barn, and be considered an interesting item." The memoir, dropped from the 1851 and succeeding editions, was later reprinted in the posthumous collection *At Home and Abroad* (New York, 1872), pp. 9-36.

6. All the correspondence relating to the publication of *Swallow Barn* is quoted from the KP, Correspondence with Publishers.

7. KP, Letters to Elizabeth, Vol. I, December 25, 1832.

8. Except where otherwise noted, all quotations of reviews of *Swallow Barn* are drawn from this source—the volume which Kennedy called "Scraps."

9. *New England Magazine,* III (July, 1832), 77.

10. KP, Letters to John Pendleton Kennedy, Vol. XVII, May 23, 1832.

11. Quoted by Jay B. Hubbell, *The South in American Literature* (Durham, 1954), p. 492n.

12. KP, Letters to John Pendleton Kennedy, Vol. VIII, February 24, 1833.

13. Cooper's words are quoted in a letter from Carey to Kennedy, January 15, 1834, in KP, Correspondence with Publishers.

14. *Swallow Barn* was first published in a two-volume edition by Carey & Lea in 1832. The second, or revised, edition was issued by George P. Putnam in 1851, with twenty illustrations by David Strother. Kennedy did not extensively alter his work. He excised the long essay on Captain John Smith, reworked the openings of several of the earlier chapters, and changed the phraseology at a number of points throughout. As he remarked in his 1851 preface, his aim had been "improvement" of the text and not any basic recasting of the book. The quotation from the 1832 edition is on pp. vii-viii; that from the 1851 edition on pp. 10-11.

15. See Bohner, pp. 73 ff. Osborne's discussion is in his introduction to the Hafner edition of *Swallow Barn* (New York, 1962). I believe that Osborne overemphasizes the specific satire of Irving's *Bracebridge Hall* and does not sufficiently consider other ele-

ments. Hubbell's comment is in *The South in American Literature*, p. 492.

16. *Swallow Barn*, p. 29. My quotations follow Kennedy's revised text of 1851; subsequent page references will be included in the body of my discussion. The text published by Hafner is a photocopy of an 1853 reprinting of the 1851 Putnam edition; it is, currently, the most conveniently available text for the student.

17. Bohner and Osborne list the actual persons from whom Kennedy may have drawn details. Bohner also points out that the autobiographical fragment in the KP written in 1825 contains a number of portrait sketches similar in manner to the Theophrastian "characters" of the seventeenth century; four of these were incorporated in *Swallow Barn*. See Bohner, pp. 81 ff.

18. For Kennedy's use of folklore elements, see Warren E. Roberts, "Some Folksong References in Kennedy's *Swallow Barn*," *Southern Folklore Quarterly*, XVII (December, 1953), 249-54.

19. William R. Taylor, in his *Cavalier and Yankee* (New York, Anchor Books, 1963), p. 159, comments: "Kennedy's Old Dominion, like Paulding's Southlands and Wirt's Old Virginia, began as a jest. He was finally no better able than others to sustain the jest, but in his first book the 'mirthful mood,' as he called it, prevailed."

20. As I have noted, Kennedy dropped the long memoir of Smith from the 1851 edition, but he kept the incident in the Swallow Barn library and Littleton's comments on Smith.

21. See note 5, above.

22. KP, Journal No. 1, December 16, 1830.

23. KP, My Notebook for Scraps and Thoughts. Kennedy's views on emancipation, incidentally, drew from Simms an admiring letter after the appearance of the revised version of *Swallow Barn* in 1851 (see Mary C. Simms Oliphant, *et al.*, eds., *The Letters of William Gilmore Simms*, Columbia, S. C., 1954, III, 122). But Kennedy could not have agreed with Simms' hopes for a slave-based Southern empire.

Chapter Three

1. All letters relating to the publication of *Horse-Shoe Robinson* are quoted from the KP, Correspondence with Publishers. The first edition was published by Carey, Lea & Blanchard, 1835, in two volumes; the second, revised edition was issued by George P. Putnam in 1852.

2. This and other quotations from Kennedy's journal are from the KP, Journal No. 1. Both Kennedy and his printers were incon-

sistent in their spelling of the title and of the character's name. I have adopted *Horse-Shoe Robinson* for the title and Horse Shoe for the character.

3. Kennedy's relationship with Poe is well known and is frequently discussed by Poe's biographers. See, for example, A. H. Quinn, *Edgar Allan Poe: A Critical Biography* (New York, 1941); also Bohner, pp. 193-197.

4. *Horse-Shoe Robinson,* edited by Ernest E. Leisy (New York, 1937), p. 11. All quotations are taken from this edition, which is the most readily available reprinting of Kennedy's 1852 revision (it has been reissued by the Hafner Publishing Company, New York, 1962). Hereafter page references will be included in the text. Except for a new introduction, revisions and modifications of a few sentences, and alterations in the punctuation, the 1852 text does not differ materially from that of the first edition of 1835.

5. The 1835 edition preserves the fiction that the book had been written by Mark Littleton, the narrator of *Swallow Barn.* The first version of the meeting of the author with the real Horse Shoe appears in Vol. II, pp. 295-97. When Kennedy revised the book, he transferred the account to his new preface.

6. Articles dealing with the question of the authenticity of *Horse-Shoe Robinson* are these: John R. Moore, "Kennedy's Horse Shoe Robinson: Fact or Fiction?" *American Literature,* IV (May, 1932), 160-66; Rhoda C. Ellison, "Early Alabama Interest in Southern Writers," *Alabama Review,* I (April, 1948), 101-10; Rhoda C. Ellison, "An Interview with Horse-Shoe Robinson," *American Literature,* XXXI (November, 1959), 329-32; and William S. Osborne, "John Pendleton Kennedy's *Horse Shoe Robinson*: A Novel with 'the Utmost Historical Accuracy,'" *Maryland Historical Magazine,* LIX (September 1964), 286-96.

In this last article, Osborne quotes a passage from Lyman C. Draper, *King's Mountain and Its Heroes* (Cincinnati, 1881): "Major [Edward] Musgrove had two daughters, Mary and Susan, aged respectively some twenty-five and twenty-three years, at the period of the war troubles of 1780-81. . . . [Mary] was the renowned heroine of Kennedy's popular story 'Horse-Shoe Robinson'; and in all the upcountry of South Carolina, he could not have chosen a more beautiful character in real life with which to adorn the charming pages of his historical romance." But Kennedy's Mary Musgrove is the young daughter of Allen Musgrove, a miller and a pacifist. Draper's comment is not untypical of the weaknesses in arguments attempting to prove Kennedy's "authenticity."

7. These and other quotations from Kennedy's notes on the composition of *Horse-Shoe Robinson* are drawn from the KP, Vol. No. 35, Manuscript Notes.

8. Critics have suggested such specific sources as David Ramsay's *History of South Carolina,* Alexander Garden's *Anecdotes,* and the memoirs of the war published by Alexander Graydon and William Heath. See the article by Osborne, cited in note 6, above.

9. KP, Vol. No. 35, Manuscript Notes.

10. This mystical side of Lindsay is apparently a relic of Kennedy's original idea of a "prophecy" concerning Mildred and Butler.

11. Simms's *The Partisan* (1835) deals, like Kennedy's book, with the guerilla warfare in South Carolina following the fall of Charleston in 1780. The first of seven romances which Simms devoted to the subject of the Revolution as fought in the Southern colonies, it helped to win for him the reputation of being "the Southern Cooper." Simms had planned his story for some time before *Horse-Shoe Robinson* appeared, and the similarities between the two books must be considered coincidental.

12. The source for this and other letters about *Horse-Shoe Robinson* is the KP, Letters to John Pendleton Kennedy.

13. Poe's review appeared in the *Southern Literary Messenger,* I (May, 1835), 522-36.

14. These quotations from reviews are drawn from the KP, the volume labelled "Scraps."

15. William Gilmore Simms, review of *Horse-Shoe Robinson, Southern Quarterly Review,* New Series, VI (July, 1852), 203-20. See also Simms's letter to Kennedy in the Simms *Letters,* III, 183.

16. The clipping, dated September 15, 1852, is identified in Kennedy's hand as being taken from the New Orleans *Delta.* It is preserved in the KP, Ego Clippings.

17. KP, Journal No. 5, September 26, 1841.

18. KP, Scraps. The clipping is undated.

19. For further discussion of the phase of Kennedy's public career covered in this section, see Bohner, pp. 115-28.

Chapter Four

1. KP, Journal No. 1, September 29, 1835.

2. These manuscript notes are preserved in the KP, Vol. No. 35, Manuscript Notes.

3. It may have been even earlier that Kennedy made this isolated jotting in Journal No. 2: "A singular being was brought in

and seated upon the table where a party of revellers were employed over their cups. This was Billy of the Bowl—a decrepit creature who had no legs and as a substitute he was placed in a large wooden bowl with which by means of two crutches he steered himself along.—His body was full grown—his head large,—heavy shock of hair —a very intelligent face.—He was a great favourite on account of his wit which was singularly active. He was shrewd and sarcastic—"

4. Kennedy lined out the portion of this sentence enclosed in brackets.

5. All the correspondence relating to publication of *Rob of the Bowl* is quoted from KP, Correspondence with Publishers.

6. KP, Letters to Elizabeth, Vol. II, September 15, 1838.

7. *Rob of the Bowl* was first issued by Lea & Blanchard, 1838, in two volumes. A revised edition was published by G. P. Putnam & Company in 1854; I have adopted this text as the basis for my discussion, and the page references included in the text are to it. There was a reprinting of *Rob* issued by A. L. Burt, New York, early in the twentieth century; this is a badly abridged text and is worthless for scholarly purposes.

Since I have written this chapter, however, a new edition of *Rob* has been prepared by William S. Osborne and published by College and University Press (New Haven, Connecticut, 1965).

8. See, for example, a letter from Robert Gilmor, dated November 4, 1835, in KP, Letters to John Pendleton Kennedy, Vol. VI. Gilmor remarks that he is sending a list of the names of civil and military officers of Maryland in the seventeenth century which might be of use in the new book. Kennedy was aided in his researches by David Ridgely, the state librarian, whom he thanks in his preface. Some of the documents which he borrowed remained among his papers until 1895, when they were finally discovered and returned to the Maryland Historical Society. For a fuller account, see Bohner, p. 102. Kennedy's own account of some of his researches is given in his "A Legend of Maryland," discussed in Chapter 6 of this study.

Some note should be taken here with respect to the actual religious situation in Maryland. Kennedy does not dwell on the fact that the Toleration Act, passed by the Assembly in 1649, guaranteed liberty of conscience only to believers in the divinity of Christ; denial of the Trinity was considered a capital offense. Freedom of religious practice, then, was only relative.

9. Draft for a revised preface to *Rob of the Bowl,* KP, Vol. No. 55, Miscellaneous Notes. Kennedy apparently never sent a copy to his publishers, and the 1854 edition reprinted the 1838 preface without change.

10. See Bohner, p. 106.

11. Letter dated March 25, 1839, in KP, Correspondence with Publishers.

12. These quotations are drawn from materials preserved in the KP, Scraps.

13. The letter, written to Mrs. Henry V. Somerville from Washington in 1839, is quoted in an article, "He Lives in His Books," Baltimore *Sun,* June 12, 1910, p. 12. In an unfinished draft of a preface for the new edition of 1854, Kennedy confessed that *Rob*'s "first reception by the public did not correspond with the expectations of the author." However, the *Sun* article reports that *Rob* can "today [1910] be found on the accessible counters of Baltimore bookstores, a book in frequent and steady demand."

14. Based on table in Lyle H. Wright, *American Fiction: 1774-1850* (San Marino, Calif., 1948), pp. 317-18. It is possible that two earlier romances by Simms had some influence on the characters and plot of *Rob of the Bowl.* Simms's best-known creation, Captain Porgy, is a figure somewhat like Dauntrees, though both are clearly reminiscent of Falstaff. Porgy first figured in *The Partisan* (1835). In Simms's *The Yemassee* (also 1835) there is a hero about whose true identity there is a mystery and a captain of a pirate ship who kidnaps the sweetheart of the hero. But both Simms and Kennedy might have found such staples of romance in any number of places.

Chapter Five

1. All comments concerning the composition of *Quodlibet* are drawn from the KP, Journal No. 5. Various early notes and draft versions are in the KP, Vol. No. 35, Manuscript Notes.

2. In addition to these comments about social order in the United States, set down in his journal, Kennedy wrote a number of essays about American society which were published posthumously in *At Home and Abroad*—a volume of miscellaneous writings prepared by Henry T. Tuckerman when he edited the author's collected works in 1871-1872.

3. *Quodlibet* (Philadelphia, 1840), p. 45. Further references in the text are to this edition. "Quodlibet" means "what pleases" or "what you please."

4. *Main Currents in American Thought* (New York, 1927), II, 55.

5. KP, Letters to His Mother and His Uncle, letter dated October 10, 1840.

6. *Quodlibet* (Philadelphia, 1860), pp. v-vi, viii.

7. For a full discussion of this period, see Bohner, Chapters VIII and IX.

8. Bohner, pp. 153-54.

9. KP, Journal No. 5, December 24, 1843. All quotations relating to the composition of the *Life of Wirt* are from this journal.

10. KP, Journal No. 7a.

11. KP, Journal No. 7a, December 14, 1849. The punctuation has been slightly altered for clarity.

12. KP, Journal No. 7e, April, 1851, p. 218. I have slightly edited this entry for clarity.

13. KP, Ego Clippings.

14. The review, by George S. Bryan, appeared in the *Southern Quarterly Review*, New Series, V (January, 1852), 71-86.

15. KP, Letters of John Pendleton Kennedy, Vol. III, February 6, 1852. The text is difficult to read in several places.

16. Simms, *Letters*, III, 123.

17. *Ibid.*, p. 183.

Chapter Six

1. KP, Journal No. 5. Kennedy copied this letter into his journal under the date March 18, 1846.

2. KP, Letters of John Pendleton Kennedy, Vol. III, February 29, 1852.

3. For a full discussion of Kennedy's later years, see Bohner, Chapters XI and XII.

4. KP, Letters of John Pendleton Kennedy, Vol. V, March 21, 1857.

5. KP, Journal No. 7k, January 15, 1859.

6. The *Southern Literary Messenger* version appeared in Vol. XXIV (March, 1857), pp. 223-35. The "Legend" was reprinted by Tuckerman in the posthumous collection *At Home and Abroad* (New York, 1872), pp. 37-87. I have used this latter text.

7. "Legend," p. 37.

8. Quoted in Tuckerman, pp. 470-71.

9. *Tributes to the Memory of the Hon. John Pendleton Kennedy* (Cambridge, Massachusetts, 1871), p. 13.

10. KP, Letters of John Pendleton Kennedy, Vol. III, April 8, 1852.

11. See, for example, Alexander Cowie, *op. cit.*, p. 269.

12. *Quodlibet* (Philadelphia, 1860), pp. vi-vii.

13. KP, Journal No. 7i, October 25, 1854.

Selected Bibliography

PRIMARY SOURCES

1. *Principal Works*

Swallow Barn, or A Sojourn in the Old Dominion. Philadelphia: Carey & Lea, 1832; New York: G. P. Putnam & Company, 1851. (Modern editions: New York: Harcourt, Brace & Company, 1929, ed. by Jay B. Hubbell; New York: Hafner Publishing Company, 1962, intro. and notes by William Osborne. This latter edition is a photographic reproduction of the text of 1851.)

Horse-Shoe Robinson: A Tale of the Tory Ascendancy. Philadelphia: Carey, Lea & Blanchard, 1835; New York: George P. Putnam, 1852. (Modern editions: New York: American Book Company, 1937, ed. by Ernest E. Leisy; New York: Hafner Publishing Company, 1962—a reprint of the Leisy edition.)

Rob of the Bowl: A Legend of St. Inigoe's. Philadelphia: Lea & Blanchard, 1838; New York: G. P. Putnam & Company, 1854. (Modern edition: New Haven, Connecticut: College and University Press, 1965, intro. and notes by William S. Osborne. This edition follows the text of the second publication [1854].)

Quodlibet . . . Philadelphia: Lea & Blanchard, 1840; Philadelphia: J. B. Lippincott & Company, 1860.

Memoirs of the Life of William Wirt. Philadelphia: Lea & Blanchard, 1849.

2. *Collected Edition*

The Collected Works of John Pendleton Kennedy. New York: G. P. Putnam & Sons, 1871-1872. 10 vols. Contains the five works listed above, the *Life* by Tuckerman (see below), and three volumes of miscellanies edited by Tuckerman: *At Home and Abroad, Political and Official Papers,* and *Occasional Addresses.*

3. *Manuscripts*

The most important collection is the Kennedy Papers, which the author left to the Peabody Institute Library, Baltimore, Maryland. There are numerous documents in these chief categories: (1) journals, 35 vols., covering the years 1829-1869; (2) letters, 33 vols., including letters by and to Kennedy for the years 1812-1870; (3) manuscripts of all Kennedy's published works; (4) literary miscellanies, including notes and drafts, commonplace books, etc.; (5) scrapbooks of newspaper clippings, including many contemporary reviews of Kennedy's books. For a full account of this collection, see the article by Lloyd W. Griffin, listed below.

SECONDARY SOURCES

1. *Books*

Bohner, Charles H. *John Pendleton Kennedy: Gentleman from Baltimore*. Baltimore: The Johns Hopkins Press, 1961. Based largely on the extensive holdings of Kennedy papers in the Peabody Library, this is a thorough modern biography. Emphasizes Kennedy the man of public affairs rather than the author.

Cowie, Alexander. *The Rise of the American Novel*. New York: American Book Company, 1948. Contains an eleven-page discussion of Kennedy's principal works of fiction and is useful for seeing the author against the background of his own period.

Gwathmey, Edward M. *John Pendleton Kennedy*. New York: Thomas Nelson & Sons, 1931. Not of primary importance; adds little to Tuckerman (see below) and is occasionally inaccurate.

Hubbell, Jay B. *The South in American Literature, 1607-1900*. Durham: Duke University Press, 1954. A fifteen-page discussion summarizes the main biographical facts and analyzes the chief works of fiction. Important for understanding Kennedy against the background of other creative writing in the South during his lifetime.

Leisy, Ernest E. *The American Historical Novel*. Norman, Okla.: University of Oklahoma Press, 1950. Contains only brief remarks about Kennedy's works, but may be consulted for information about the development of historical fiction in the United States.

Oliphant, Mary C. Simms, *et al.*, eds. *The Letters of William Gilmore Simms*. Columbia: University of South Carolina Press, 1952-1956. 5 vols. Includes a number of valuable letters from Simms to Kennedy and is generally helpful for an understanding of the life of the literary man in the South.

Osborne, William Stewart. *John Pendleton Kennedy: A Study of his Literary Career*. Unpublished doctoral dissertation, Columbia

University, 1960. Like Bohner's book, this study is based chiefly on the materials in the Peabody Library, but it has much fuller discussions of Kennedy's literary works and his relationships with other writers of his day.

PARRINGTON, VERNON L. *Main Currents in American Thought.* New York: Harcourt, Brace & Company, 1927. Vol. II. Not always accurate in its remarks about Kennedy's life, this discussion is nonetheless a milestone in the modern revaluation of the author.

PRETZER, WALLACE LEONARD, *Eighteenth-Century Literary Conventions in the Fictional Style of John Pendleton Kennedy.* Unpublished doctoral dissertation, University of Michigan, 1963. The purpose of this study is "to characterize Kennedy's fictional style in the light of Fielding's and Sterne's styles."

SEMMES, JOHN E. *John H. B. Latrobe and His Times.* Baltimore: Norman, Remington Company, 1917. Biography of a friend of Kennedy's which is valuable for its background of the Baltimore in which Kennedy lived.

TAYLOR, WILLIAM R. *Cavalier and Yankee.* New York: Anchor Books, 1963. Chapter V, "A Squire of Change Alley: The Plantation Legend and the Aristocratic Impulse," is one of the most provocative recent discussions of Kennedy's contributions to Southern legend.

Tributes to the Memory of the Hon. John Pendleton Kennedy. Cambridge, Mass.: J. Wilson & Son, 1871. A memorial volume made up of tributes by James Russell Lowell and others.

TUCKERMAN, HENRY T. *The Life of John Pendleton Kennedy.* New York: G. P. Putnam & Sons, 1871. The "official" life, written by Kennedy's chief literary executor. Contains valuable material now unavailable elsewhere, but has been largely superseded by the publication of Bohner's biography.

2. *Essays*

These are the most useful among recent articles for the student of Kennedy's literary career. For fuller listings see Lewis Leary, *Articles on American Literature, 1900-1950* (Durham: Duke University Press, 1954); since 1950, the bibliographies published in the journals *PMLA* (Modern Language Association) and *American Literature.* (A few other articles not listed here are recorded in the Notes and References section.)

BOHNER, CHARLES H. "'As Much History as . . . Invention': John P. Kennedy's *Rob of the Bowl,*" *William and Mary Quarterly,* XVII (July, 1960), 329-340. This and the following three articles are slightly expanded versions of materials contained in Bohner's book (see above).

———. "J. P. Kennedy's *Quodlibet*: Whig Counterattack," *American Quarterly,* XIII (Spring, 1961), 84-92.

———. "*Swallow Barn*: John P. Kennedy's Chronicle of Virginia Society," *Virginia Magazine of History and Biography,* LXVIII (July, 1960), 317-30.

———. "*The Red Book,* 1819-21, A Satire on Baltimore Society," *Maryland Historical Magazine,* LI (September, 1956), 175-87.

ELLISON, RHODA COLEMAN. "An Interview with Horse-Shoe Robinson," *American Literature,* XXXI (November, 1959), 329-32. Decribes a visit made by the Alabama editor A. B. Meek to the titular hero of Kennedy's novel in 1838.

GRIFFIN, LLOYD W. "The John Pendleton Kennedy Manuscripts," *Maryland Historical Magazine,* XLVIII (December, 1953), 327-36. A full account of the papers held by the Peabody Institute Library, Baltimore.

MOORE, JOHN R. "Kennedy's Horse-Shoe Robinson: Fact or Fiction?" *American Literature,* IV (May, 1932), 160-66. Concludes that Kennedy's romance is "not an elaboration of the recollections of Horse-Shoe Robinson."

OSBORNE, WILLIAM S. "John Pendleton Kennedy's *Horse Shoe Robinson*: A Novel with 'the Utmost Historical Accuracy,'" *Maryland Historical Magazine,* LIX (September, 1964), 286-96. Cites parallels between Kennedy's novel and sources such as Alexander Garden's *Anecdotes* and David Ramsey's *History of South Carolina* in an attempt to prove Kennedy's "reliance on real people for his characters and his use of factual material to supply his background."

UHLER, JOHN E. "Kennedy's Novels and his Posthumous Works," *American Literature,* III (January, 1932), 471-79. Asserts that Kennedy's "Legend of Maryland" ranks, "in originality if not in concentration of effect, with Poe's mystery stories."

Index

Index